WHY SHOULD WE READ AND DISCUSS THE BOOK OF ISAIAH?

Anyone who really wants to understand the Bible in depth has to engage the book of Isaiah. In sheer volume of material alone, Isaiah makes up a substantial portion of the Scriptures. It's as long as all of Paul's letters combined. Even more significantly, many vital truths about God are disclosed for the first time in the book—truths about who God is and about what God's plans are for the redemption of humanity and all of creation. As a result, Isaiah is one of the most influential books within the rest of the Bible. The New Testament writers quote from it more often than from any other book. Beyond all this, it has also exerted a strong cultural influence beyond the Bible. It's the source of popular metaphors and sayings, such as the idea of "beating swords into plowshares," and "the wolf lying down with the lamb," and it has inspired artworks and musical compositions down through the centuries, such as Edward Hicks's paintings of *The Peaceable Kingdom* and much of Handel's oratorio *Messiah*. So this is simply an indispensable book to engage and appreciate.

At the same time, however, Isaiah is one of the most difficult books in the Bible to understand. There are a number of reasons for this.

- For one thing, it's unique among the biblical books in that it was occasioned by two different crises in the life of the nation of Israel, 150 years apart. In addition to addressing these crises, it also looks farther ahead to God's ultimate purposes in the world.
- For another thing, the major sections of the book aren't in

chronological sequence. Rather, they oscillate back and forth between these two periods. (See the chart on page 10.)

- Even within sections that speak to a given period, the materials aren't arranged the way they would be in the works we know today. They're not in a logical or thematic progression. Instead, there's sharp alteration between different moods, themes, and messages.
- Finally, most of the book consists of prophetic oracles, a particular kind of poetry or song that has no real equivalent today and which is unfamiliar to most readers as a result.

For all of these reasons, anyone who tries to read straight through the book of Isaiah will likely become lost and confused, and potentially pretty frustrated as well. The grandeur of many of the passages keeps readers going, hoping for more (and they find it), but they often get no understanding of the book as a whole.

To overcome these difficulties and help readers understand and appreciate this vital work within the Scriptures, this study guide will take a different approach. The book of Isaiah is essentially a collection of poems, songs, and stories. They were put together, for reasons that will become clear in the sessions ahead, in an order we would not expect today. But as in the case of any biblical book that is a collection of independent compositions (like Psalms), rather than a single composition itself (like Esther), it's necessary first to understand the parts, and then understand the whole from the parts, rather than working in the opposite direction.

To help today's readers do this, this guide will take up the materials within Isaiah in a different order from the one in which they appear in the book. It will take up the passages in the book in their historical order, explaining their historical contexts, so that readers can ultimately also appreciate their literary contexts—that is, their placement in a particular location within the entire collection.

The book of Isaiah is a bit like the kind of trophy case you'd find in the front hallway of a school. The trophies, awards, and plaques in these cases usually aren't arranged in historical order, from left to right. Instead, the tallest trophy will likely be in the middle, with shorter trophies on each side, and even shorter ones toward the edges of the case—regardless of when they were won. Photos and plaques will be hung on the back wall where there is space and visibility, but not necessarily right behind trophies from the same era. The overall goal is to create a pleasing and appealing visual arrangement. In the same way, the poems, stories, and songs in the book of Isaiah are arranged not historically but artistically. Prophetic responses to significant challenges that the people of God faced at different times are blended together into an overall message. This study guide will help you appreciate this arrangement, engage the materials within it, and so grasp the message of this giant, influential book within the Bible. Isaiah will always be a difficult book to understand, and it will require effort and perseverance to work through this guide. But if you're up for a challenge that will pay very rich rewards, and particularly if you're familiar with the format of these guides from using other titles in the series, then come aboard for a tour of the vast, fascinating landscape of this monumental inspired work.

UNDERSTANDING THE BOOKS OF THE BIBLE

ISAIAH

Also available in the
UNDERSTANDING THE BOOKS OF THE BIBLE series:

Biblical Apocalypses: Daniel/Revelation
Deuteronomy/Hebrews
Genesis
Job
John
Joshua/Judges/Ruth
Luke/Acts
Lyric Poetry: Psalms/Song of Songs/Lamentations
Paul's Journey Letters: Thessalonians/Corinthians/
Galatians/Romans
Paul's Prison Letters: Colossians/Ephesians/Philemon/
Philippians/Timothy/Titus
Wisdom: Proverbs/Ecclesiastes/James

Future releases:

Mark
Prophets Before the Exile: Amos/Hosea/Micah/Zephaniah/
Nahum/Habakkuk

UNDERSTANDING THE BOOKS OF THE BIBLE

ISAIAH

Christopher R. Smith

An imprint of InterVarsity Press
Downers Grove, Illinois

InterVarsity Press
P.O. Box 1400, Downers Grove, IL 60515-1426
World Wide Web: www.ivpress.com
E-mail: email@ivpress.com

InterVarsity Press® is the book-publishing division of InterVarsity Christian Fellowship/USA®, a movement of students and faculty active on campus at hundreds of universities, colleges and schools of nursing in the United States of America, and a member movement of the International Fellowship of Evangelical Students. For information about local and regional activities, write Public Relations Dept., InterVarsity Christian Fellowship/USA, 6400 Schroeder Rd., P.O. Box 7895, Madison, WI 53707-7895, or visit the IVCF website at <www.intervarsity.org>.

Design: Cindy Kiple
Images: © PK-Photos/iStockphoto

ISBN 978-0-8308-5811-8

Printed in the United States of America ∞

green press INITIATIVE *InterVarsity Press is committed to protecting the environment and to the responsible use of natural resources. As a member of Green Press Initiative we use recycled paper whenever possible. To learn more about the Green Press Initiative, visit <www.greenpressinitiative.org>.*

P *20 19 18 17 16 15 14 13 12 11 10 9 8 7 6 5 4 3 2 1*
Y *30 29 28 27 26 25 24 23 22 21 20 19 18 17 16 15 14 13*

CONTENTS

HOW THESE STUDY GUIDES ARE DIFFERENT

Did you know you could read and study the Bible without using any chapters or verses? The books of the Bible are real "books." They're meant to be experienced the same way other books are: as exciting, interesting works that keep you turning pages right to the end and then make you want to go back and savor each part. The UNDERSTANDING THE BOOKS OF THE BIBLE series of study guides will help you do that with the Bible.

These guides are especially designed to be used with *The Books of the Bible*, an edition of the Scriptures from Biblica that takes out the chapter and verse numbers and presents the biblical books in their natural form. Here's what people are saying about reading the Bible this way:

> I love it. I find myself understanding Scripture in a new way, with a fresh lens, and I feel spiritually refreshed as a result. I learn much more through stories being told and, with this new format, I feel the truth of the story come alive for me.

> Reading Scripture this way flows beautifully. I don't miss the chapter and verse numbers. I like them gone. They got in the way.

> I've been a reader of the Bible all of my life. But after reading just a few pages without chapters and verses, I was amazed at what I'd been missing all these years.

For more information about *The Books of the Bible* or to obtain a copy of this specially designed edition, visit www.Biblica.com/thebooks. Watch the site for a four-volume set comprising the entire Bible in this format, coming soon. (Note: In general, the guides in this series are designed so that they can also be used with any other version or translation. But for the best possible experience with this guide to Isaiah, it is strongly recommended that you use *The Books of the Bible*, or at least a copy of the New International Version.)

For people who are used to chapters and verses, reading and studying the Bible without them may take a little getting used to. It's like when you get a new smart phone, or move from using a laptop to a tablet. You have to unlearn some old ways of doing things and learn some new ways. But it's not too long until you catch on to how the new system works and you find you can do a lot of things you couldn't do before.

Here are some of the ways you and your group will have a better experience of the Scriptures by using these study guides.

YOU'LL UNDERSTAND WHOLE BOOKS

Imagine going to a friend's house to watch a movie you've never seen before. After only a couple of scenes, your friend stops the film and says, "So, tell me what you think of it so far." When you give your best shot at a reply, based on the little you've seen, your friend says, "You know, there's a scene in another movie that always makes me think of this one." He switches to a different movie and before you know it, you're watching a scene from the middle of another film.

Who would ever try to watch a movie this way? Yet many study guides take this approach to the Bible. They have you read a few paragraphs from one book, then jump to a passage in another book. The UNDERSTANDING THE BOOKS OF THE BIBLE series doesn't do that. Instead, these study guides focus on understanding the message and meaning of one book. This guide will take you through the book of Isaiah, equipping you to understand its meaning and message for the people of its own time, so that you can then appreciate how it speaks to people of all times.

YOU'LL APPROACH BOOKS ON THEIR OWN TERMS

You won't go chapter-by-chapter through Isaiah, because the chapter divisions in the Bible often come at the wrong places and break up natural sections. Did you know that the chapter divisions used in most modern Bibles were added more than a thousand years after the biblical books were written? And that the verse numbers were added more than three centuries after that? If you grew up with the chapter-and-verse system, it may feel like part of the inspired Word of God. But it's not. Those little numbers aren't holy, and when you read and study Isaiah without them, you'll hear its message more clearly than ever before.

Session 1 is an overview that will introduce you to the major parts of the book of Isaiah. This will equip you to consider its individual sections in the sessions that follow. The parts of the book and the historical situations they address are illustrated in the chart on page 10. To help you get a feel for where you are in the book's natural flow, sessions will be headed by a visual cue, like this:

Book of Isaiah > Part Two: Prophecies Against the Nations > Egypt

YOU'LL DECIDE FOR YOURSELVES WHAT TO DISCUSS

In each session of this study guide there are many options for discussion. While each session could be completed by a group in about an hour and a half, any one of the questions could lead to an involved conversation. There's no need to cut the conversation short to try to "get through it all." As a group leader, you can read through all the questions ahead of time and decide which one(s) to begin with, and what order to take them up in. If you do get into an involved discussion of one question, you can leave out some of the others. Or, you can extend the study over more than one meeting if you do want to cover them all. Isaiah is a long and complex book, and in many cases you may find that you do want to devote more than one meeting of your group to a single session.

TOGETHER, YOU'LL TELL THE STORY

Each session gives suggestions for how the passage or passages you'll be discussing can be read in a way that brings out their form and meaning. In certain sessions you'll read narratives out loud in parts like a play. In other sessions you'll recite the book's oracles in ways that bring out their distinctive shape and message. This community oral reading of the Bible is a spiritual discipline that allows people to take the Scriptures more deeply to heart. This discipline is very timely in a culture that's increasingly characterized by a "new orality."

If you're using *The Books of The Bible*, you'll find that the natural sections it marks off by white space match up in most cases with the sections of the reading. If you're using another edition of the Bible, some of these sections may be more difficult to distinguish because translations differ in their portrayals of where oracles begin and end. Nevertheless, you should still be able to follow along because the readings are also identified in this guide by their opening lines, or by some other means designed to make them clear.

EVERYBODY WILL PARTICIPATE

There's plenty of opportunity for everyone in the group to participate. Everyone can take turns reading the passages that you'll be considering. Group members can also read the session introduction aloud, or the discussion questions. As a leader, you can easily involve quiet people by giving them these opportunities. And everyone will feel that they can speak up and answer the questions, because they're not looking for "right answers." Instead, they invite the group to work together to understand the Bible.

YOU'LL ALL SHARE DEEPLY

The discussion questions will invite you to share deeply about your ideas and experiences. The answers to these questions can't be found just by "looking them up." They require reflection on the meaning of each saying, in the wider context of the book, in light of your personal experience. These aren't the kinds of abstract, academic questions that make the discussion feel

like a test. Instead, they'll connect the Bible passage to your life in practical, personal, relational ways.

To create a climate of trust where this kind of deep sharing is encouraged, here are a couple of ground rules that your group should agree to at its first meeting:

Confidentiality. Group members agree to keep what is shared in the group strictly confidential. "What's said in the group stays in the group."

Respect. Group members will treat other members with respect at all times, even when disagreeing over ideas.

HOW TO LEAD GROUP STUDIES USING THIS GUIDE

Each session has three basic parts:

Introduction

Have a member of your group read the introduction to the session out loud to everyone. Then give group members the chance to ask questions about the introduction, and offer their own thoughts and examples.

Reading

Have people read out loud the passage(s) of the book of Isaiah that you'll be discussing. The study guide will offer suggestions for various ways you can do this for each session. In many cases reading and discussion will be combined.

Discussion Questions

Most questions are introduced with some observations. These may give some background to the history and culture of the ancient world, or explain where you are in the flow of the book. After these observations there are suggested discussion questions. Many of them have multiple parts that are really just different ways of getting at an issue.

You don't have to discuss the questions in the order they appear in the study guide. You can choose to spend your time exploring just one or two questions, and not do the others. Or you can have shorter discussion of each question so that you do cover all of them. As the group leader, before the meeting you should read the questions and the observations that introduce them, and decide which ones you want to emphasize.

When you get to a given question, have someone read aloud the observations and the question. As you answer the question, interact with the observations (you can agree or disagree with them) in light of your reading from the Bible. Use only part of the question to get at the issue from one angle, or use all of the parts, as you choose.

For Further Reading and Discussion

At the end of some sessions, other passages in the book of Isaiah that are related to the ones you've just considered will be suggested for further reading and discussion. Your group can consider some of these if it wants to and has time. Individuals can also read and reflect on them on their own. Because the book is so long and complex, it's not possible to treat all of its passages within the sessions themselves in a study guide of this length. But any parts of the book not discussed within a session will be introduced this way at the end of a session.

TIPS FOR HOME GROUPS, SUNDAY SCHOOL CLASSES, COMMUNITY BIBLE EXPERIENCES, AND INDIVIDUAL USE

If you're using this guide in a *home group*, you may want to begin each meeting (or at least some meetings) by having dinner together. You may also want to have a time of singing and prayer before or after the study. (A few of the sessions will suggest songs you can sing or listen to that are based on the passages in Isaiah that they cover. If you want to use these suggestions, *look for the songs ahead of time*, for example, by finding videos of them on the Internet, or getting someone to bring a recorded version of them to your meeting, or having the words and music printed out for people to sing and for someone to play on a piano, guitar, etc.)

If you're using this guide in a *Sunday school class*, you may want to have a time of singing and prayer before or after the study.

This study guide can also be used in connection with a *community Bible experience* of the book of Isaiah. If you're using it in this way:

- Encourage people to read each session's Scripture passage by themselves early in the week.
- Do each session in midweek small groups.
- Invite people to write/create some response to each small-group session that could be shared in worship that weekend. These might involve poetry, journal or blog entries, artwork, dramas, videos, and so on.
- During the weekend worship services, let people share these responses, and have preaching on the topic of the session that was studied that week. Speakers can gather comments they've heard from people and draw on their own reflections to sum up the church's experience of that session.
- The following week will be devoted to the next session in the same way.

This guide can also be used for *individual study*. You can write out your responses to the questions in a notebook or journal. (However, we really encourage reading and studying the Bible in community!)

• • • • •

You may find it helpful to read the introduction to Isaiah in The Books of the Bible *before doing session 1.*

THE ASSYRIAN CRISIS

MAJOR PARTS OF THE BOOK OF ISAIAH

• numbers within blocks indicate sessions in this guide
• black arrows indicate the literary flow of the book

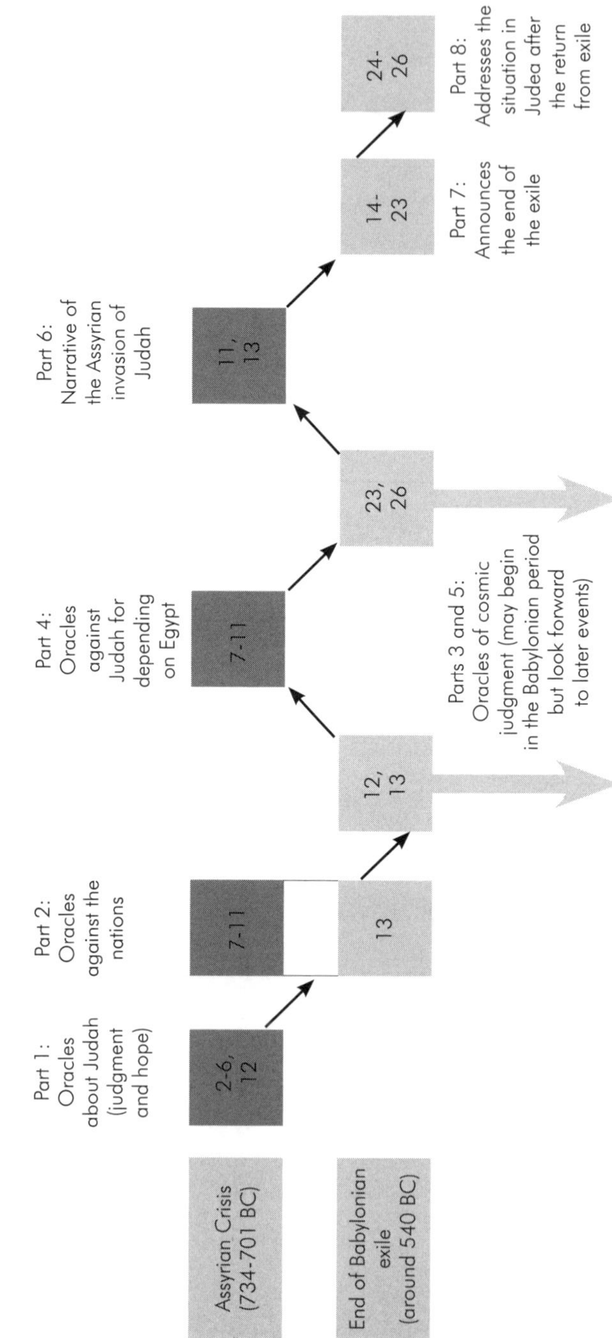

A version of this chart first appeared in *Bible Study Magazine*, March/April 2010, pp. 26-27.

SESSION 1

HOW THE BOOK OF ISAIAH IS PUT TOGETHER

Book of Isaiah (Overview)

Before doing this session, have someone read aloud the material entitled "Why Should We Read and Discuss the Book of Isaiah?" at the start of this guide.

INTRODUCTION

Our goal in this study guide will be to take up the various passages in the book of Isaiah in an order that will enable readers to appreciate its overall meaning and message. We'll begin in this session with an overview of the book, so that as particular passages are discussed in the sessions ahead, you can locate them readily. Isaiah has eight major sections, and once you recognize them, you can find your way around within the book relatively simply. In this session you'll be introduced to the first six sections so that you can appreciate how the book responds to the first of the crises in the life of the nation that inspired it. Later in this guide you'll be introduced to the last two sections, which address the second crisis.

It would be only too easy to use the traditional chapter numbers to identify the passages and sections in the book of Isaiah. But this wouldn't give you an understanding of its contents and structure, which you will need to appreciate its message. So instead you will learn about its structure by skimming through it, marking its major sections as you go along, and stopping to read specific passages that explain important aspects of its historical background.

SKIMMING, READING, AND DISCUSSION

Note: For this exercise, if you're not using The Books of the Bible, *you should at least use an edition of the Scriptures that prints Isaiah's oracles as poetry (line by line) and the narratives in the book as prose (in block type), rather than printing the whole book as prose.*

Have different members of your group take turns reading the explanatory material below.

Have someone read the heading to the book (the first sentence), which describes when and where Isaiah lived and prophesied.

Look at the chart on page 25 and see when the rulers of his time reigned. Look at the map on page 24 and find the kingdom of Judah. At this time the original kingdom of Israel had been divided into two parts. The southern one was called Judah and the northern one was still known as Israel.

While Isaiah lived in the southern kingdom of Judah, he still considered the northern kingdom of Israel an essential part of God's people. And so, as you'll see, he often spoke to the whole nation at once, calling it Israel or Jacob. (A man named Jacob, who was later renamed Israel, was the founding patriarch of the nation.) Isaiah saw these two kingdoms as "the two houses of Israel," as he describes them in one of his oracles.

1 In your Bible, in some way mark the place right after this heading as the start of "Part One." (You can write this in the margin, stick a Post-It Note onto the page, write down the page number, etc.) In *The Books of the Bible*, you'll see that a wide space is used to mark the start of this and every major section in Isaiah.

Slowly leaf through this first section, noticing that it consists mostly of relatively short poems. There will be small spaces between them. If your Bible has headings, they'll appear before small groups of these poems.

Skim forward several pages to the place where two short stretches of block type appear. (They both begin, "In that day . . .") These illustrate how prophets like Isaiah sometimes spoke in prose (descriptive language), even though they most often used poetry to make their messages vivid and memorable. (If you are using a different version of the Bible, you'll see that translators don't always agree about which passages are prose and which are poetry.)

See how the next poem, right after the second stretch of block type, begins: "I will sing for the one I love a song about his vineyard." Language like this suggests that many of these poems may actually be the lyrics to songs. It shows us that another way the prophets made sure their message spread and had an impact was by setting their oracles to music.

➲ Question for group discussion: If you had an important message that you wanted as many people as possible to hear and consider today, what means would you use to get it out?

As you continue to leaf through this section, you'll come across some further prose passages. The next one you'll see begins, "In the year that King Uzziah died, I saw the Lord." This passage describes how God called Isaiah to be a prophet. We'll look at it in session 2, so make a note of its location.

The passage after that begins, "When Ahaz son of Jotham, the son of Uzziah, was king of Judah." This describes the beginning of the first crisis in the life of ancient Israel that occasioned the book of Isaiah. Have four people read this passage out loud like a play, ending where King Ahaz says, "I will not put the LORD to the test." Have the readers take these parts:

- Narrator
- The LORD (Note: In English Bibles, when LORD is written in capital letters, it stands for *Yahweh*, the name God used when he made his covenant with Israel.)
- Isaiah
- King Ahaz

As this passage continues, Isaiah makes a wonderful promise about how God will deliver the nation: "The virgin will conceive and give birth to a son, and will call him Immanuel." We'll explore the meaning of this famous promise in session 3.

The events described in this passage took place around 734 BC. The entire region was dominated by the Assyrian empire, which had reduced the various kingdoms to vassal states and made them pay regular tribute. (See map, p. 24.) Israel (called Ephraim here after its largest and most powerful tribe) and the neighboring kingdom of Aram revolted against the Assyrians and invaded Judah to try to force that kingdom to join them. (As we'll see later, their coalition also included the Philistines, Moab, and Edom.) Instead of trusting in God for protection, Ahaz, the Judean king, wanted to appeal to his Assyrian overlords to rescue him. Isaiah knew that by bringing in the Assyrians, Ahaz would create much more trouble for himself than he was already in.

Continue to skim through Part One, noting how it presents a mixture of poetry and prose, and then almost all poetry again, until you get to the place where there are two short poems that are both introduced by, "In that day you will say" (or "You will say in that day"). This is the end of Part One. In the next few sessions in this guide, we'll explore how this part of the book presents the warnings and promises that Isaiah spoke to the nation during the years of the Assyrian crisis.

2 You'll now come to the place where the book says, "A prophecy against Babylon that Isaiah son of Amoz saw." Mark this as the beginning of Part Two. This next section of the book consists of a series of prophecies that Isaiah spoke about various nations around Judah. They come from different time periods. Most of them relate to how countries in the region responded to the encroachment of the expanding Assyrian empire over a period of several decades in the second half of the eighth century BC. But the opening prophecy against Babylon actually describes the resolution of a second crisis that the book addresses, which came 150 years after this first crisis. The Babylonian empire, which succeeded the Assyrian one, conquered Judah and carried the people off into exile. This oracle describes how Babylon itself will be conquered and the people of Judah liberated. (This later situation will be explained in more detail in sessions 14 and following.) All of these prophecies against the nations, even though they come from different time periods, are collected together in Part Two to help give the book an overall unity.

Skim through this section and make a note of the various nations it addresses. You should mark the start of the following prophecies in some way: by highlighting the opening line with a marker, or making a note in the margin, etc. (You will need to find these prophecies again for sessions 7–13.) As you do, locate each of these places on the map on page 24.

- Babylon (beginning, "A prophecy against Babylon")
- Assyria ("The LORD Almighty has sworn")
- The Philistines ("This prophecy came in the year King Ahaz died")
- Moab ("A prophecy against Moab")
- Aram and Israel ("A prophecy against Damascus," the capital of Aram)
- Egypt ("Woe to the land of whirring wings"—the upper Nile region; some Bible versions call it Ethiopia)
- Egypt again ("A prophecy against Egypt")
- Babylon ("A prophecy against the Desert by the Sea")
- Dumah (a city located at a desert oasis along strategic trade routes; some versions say Edom)
- Arabia (including Dedan, Tema, and Kedar, similar cities at desert oases)
- The "Valley of Vision" (meaning Judah and its capital, Jerusalem)
- Tyre ("A prophecy against Tyre")

The messages in this section of the book show that despite the shifting fortunes of God's people, God still controls the destiny of the world and all the nations in it.

3 After the prophecy against Tyre, the book declares, "See, the LORD is going to lay waste the earth and devastate it." Mark this as the beginning of Part Three. In this section the themes of judgment and restoration that were developed in the prophecies against the nations are applied on a worldwide scale.

Skim through the first poem in this section and see how it depicts the whole world breaking up because of the wrong things its inhabitants are doing.

➲ What kinds of things might people do that actually would cause the destruction of the world?

This section of the book becomes much more hopeful after the first poem. Continue to skim through it and note how it also promises that God will bring restoration after judgment. Notice once again that much of the material consists of song lyrics. This section ends with a brief prose section that begins "in that day" and promises that God's people will be restored and "come and worship the LORD on the holy mountain in Jerusalem." You'll have the opportunity to consider the oracles in this part of the book in sessions 12 and 13.

4 After taking this cosmic, future perspective, the book returns in its next section to the down-to-earth practicalities of the Assyrian crisis. This crisis outlasted the reign of Ahaz and continued into the reign of his son Hezekiah. This section of the book, like the prophecies against the nations, addresses the international situation, but it speaks primarily to the people of Judah. Many in their royal court wanted to form an alliance with Egypt to protect them from Assyria. This section of the book pronounces six "woes" against them for not trusting in God to deliver them. A "woe" is an announcement that misfortune is coming upon someone.

Skim through this section and note where each of its main passages begins. Mark the first one as the start of Part Four. (Where the NIV says "Woe to," other translations may simply read "Ah" or "What sorrow.")

- "Woe to that wreath, the pride of Ephraim's drunkards."
- "Woe to you, Ariel, Ariel, the city where David settled!"
- "Woe to those who go to great depths to hide their plans from the LORD."
- "'Woe to the obstinate children,' declares the LORD."
- "Woe to those who go down to Egypt for help."
- "Woe to you, destroyer, you who have not been destroyed! Woe to you, betrayer, you who have not been betrayed!"

Notice that this last woe is doubled, effectively making seven woes out of six. It was a popular device of Hebrew literature to create a list or group of six things and then increase the total to seven. (For example, one traditional Hebrew proverb begins, "There are six things the LORD hates, seven that are detestable to him.") We'll consider this section of the book in sessions 7–11.

5 After pronouncing this series of woes on the people of Judah for not trusting God during the Assyrian crisis, the book returns in its next section to the later crisis in the life of the nation. Mark the beginning of Part Five where it says, "Come near, you nations, and listen; pay attention, you peoples!" Here the book speaks once again in cosmic language and looks to some more distant future events. However, the opening oracle in this section is actually spoken against Edom, another of Judah's neighbors. Edom is addressed from the perspective of the second crisis behind the book. The other oracle in this short section, which begins "The desert and the parched land will be glad," promises that the people of Judah will be brought back from their exile in Babylon.

6 Part Six contains mostly historical narratives (stories), with some poetic oracles interspersed. (This is just the opposite of what you find in the rest of the book.) Mark the beginning of this section where the book shifts from poetry to prose and reads, "In the fourteenth year of King Hezekiah's reign, Sennacherib king of Assyria attacked all the fortified cities of Judah and captured them."

These stories describe the continuation and climax of the Assyrian crisis. It's now around 701 BC. For many years Hezekiah, who has succeeded his father Ahaz as king of Judah, has appeased the Assyrians by sending tribute. But he's also been expected to worship Assyria's gods. Since he is a genuine believer in the LORD, the God of Israel, he doesn't want to do this. So he has joined a rebellious coalition led by Egypt. The Assyrians have responded by overrunning the entire region with their armies. Hezekiah is under siege in Jerusalem, one of the last cities in Judah still holding out. (This is why Isaiah says, in one of the oracles in Part One, that Jerusalem is left "like a shelter in a vineyard, like a hut in a cucumber field"—standing alone, with nothing around it. The entire Assyrian crisis, which lasted for a whole generation, provides the background to the oracles collected in Parts One and Four.)

Have three people read this account out loud like a play, beginning at the start of Part Six and reading through to the place where the Assyrian commander asks, "How then can the LORD deliver Jerusalem from my hand?" Have the readers take these parts:

- Narrator
- The Assyrian field commander

- Eliakim, Shebna, and Joah (one person can speak their lines)

(You'll find out how this story turns out in session 11.)

➲ Have you ever been in a situation like this, where you felt completely overwhelmed and could turn only to God for help? If so, describe it for the group, and tell how it turned out in the end.

➲ Now that you've gotten an overall view of the book of Isaiah, what are your initial reactions? Let each person share one or two of their strongest impressions.

In sessions 14 and following you'll be introduced to Parts Seven and Eight and learn more about the second crisis behind the book of Isaiah.

SESSION 2

GOD CALLS ISAIAH TO BE A PROPHET

Book of Isaiah > Part One > Isaiah's Calling

INTRODUCTION

You now know your way around the book of Isaiah, particularly the part dealing with the Assyrian crisis, well enough to begin getting a deeper appreciation for its message by considering its individual oracles and stories. You'll begin doing that in this session by looking at an account that comes in the middle of Part One that actually relates the earliest event recorded in the book: Isaiah's call from God to be a prophet.

This episode in Isaiah's life took place about six years before Israel and Aram invaded Judah. King Uzziah had ruled the country for fifty-two years. During his reign it had been prosperous, stable, and secure. Now this great king was being succeeded by his son Jotham, who had been his co-regent for the previous ten years. Jotham would only reign another five or six years himself before dying and leaving the people in the untested hands of his twenty-year-old son Ahaz. Meanwhile, the Assyrian empire was growing in strength and size and threatening the entire region. So along with the whole nation of Judah, a young man named Isaiah was facing an uncertain and fearful future as he went into Jerusalem's temple one day to try to find hope and reassurance by worshipping God.

READING

In session 1 you noted the place in Part One where this account of Isaiah's calling occurs. Find that place again. Have several people read the story out loud like a play. (They can leave out cues like "And I said," "He said," etc.) They should begin with "In the year that King Uzziah died, I saw the Lord" and end with "the holy seed will be the stump in the land." Have the readers take these parts:

- Narrator (Isaiah recounting a personal experience)
- Seraphs (several people can speak their chorus together; later one can speak alone to Isaiah)
- Isaiah (the character in the narrative)
- The Lord (Note: When "Lord" is not written in all capital letters, it's a translation of the Hebrew term *Adonai*, "Master.")

DISCUSSION

1 Isaiah's remarkable vision in the temple reveals that Israel's true king, the LORD Almighty, the God who has called the people into a special relationship with himself, is established on his throne above the whole world. Whatever earthly kings and their armies might attempt, it is God who ultimately determines the destinies of nations. Isaiah will never forget this vital truth throughout his career, as he continually calls the people to trust in their God rather than in the strategies they might devise or the alliances they might form.

But this glimpse of God's power and presence also leads Isaiah to an awful realization about himself. The seraphs (a special kind of angel) proclaim that the LORD is "holy, holy, holy," and that the whole earth is full of his glory. This means that every living being is continually confronted with the reality of God's purity and radiance. In response, Isaiah can only acknowledge that he is "unclean." Within the ceremonial life of the nation's covenant with the LORD, this means that he is impaired, polluted, defective, and so unfit to be used in any way connected with God.

Isaiah describes himself specifically as "a man of unclean lips." Interpreters have different ideas about why he chooses this particular part of the body (rather than, for example, his heart or mind) to represent his spiritual state. It may be because the lips express, and thus make evident, a person's innermost thoughts and intentions. Or Isaiah may be saying that he can tell he isn't pure because his lips, unlike those of the seraphs, aren't continually praising God for his holiness and glory.

➲ What's the most unforgettable worship experience you've ever had? If a vision of seraphs surrounding God's throne and calling out "Holy! Holy! Holy!" would be rated a 100, how would you rate your experience? Did it have a take-home message that you carried with you into the rest of your life?

➲ What do the things you say and think, or don't say and think, regarding God reveal about where you currently stand in relationship with him?

2 Because God wants Isaiah to be available for his service, one of the seraphs flies to him with a live coal from the altar (where sacrifices for sin were offered) and touches his lips with it. The seraph announces, "Your guilt is taken away and your sin atoned for." Isaiah has admitted his need for cleansing and forgiveness, and these are applied to the very place he used to symbolize that need.

➲ Let each person consider this question privately and only share their answer with the group if they're comfortable doing so: In what part of your life do you most need God's cleansing and forgiveness?

➲ Followers of Jesus today understand the animal sacrifices that were offered in Isaiah's time to have been symbolic acts that looked forward to the ultimate sacrifice Jesus made on the cross for the sins of the whole world. Work together as a group to make sure that everyone has a basic understanding of what Jesus' followers believe his death accomplished for them. Give anyone who isn't yet a follower of Jesus the chance to ask any questions they have about this.

3 God asks, "Who will go for us?" and Isaiah eagerly volunteers. But the assignment turns out to be a perplexing one. The new prophet is to bring messages from God to the people of Judah. But they will so persistently ignore these messages that they will become less and less able to understand what God wants. As a result, the nation will ultimately be devastated by its enemies. Only a faint glimmer of hope will remain in the end.

Even though it sounds here as if God wants the people to resist and be destroyed, this is quite unlikely. We'll see in the rest of the book of Isaiah, as we also see throughout the Scriptures, that God really wants people to respond positively to his warnings and invitations and so be rescued. Rather, the language here reflects God's knowledge of the people's confidence in their own strategies and his realization that they will choose their own way even more stubbornly when they're challenged. And so God tells Isaiah, ironically, to go and make the people even more insensible and resistant. Whatever their response, the reality of the situation needs to be proclaimed.

➲ C.S. Lewis once wrote, "It is better for the creature itself, even if it never becomes good, that it should know itself a failure."[1] Do you agree?

➲ How can we distinguish between those times when a hard truth needs to be spoken to another person, even if they're unlikely to be able to hear it, and those times when it's best to say nothing and wait for the person to become more open?

➲ Why do you think God doesn't describe the assignment he has in mind for Isaiah before he asks him whether he'll take it? Choose the answer that best expresses your thoughts, or give another answer of your own:

a. God is concerned that Isaiah won't accept if he knows all that will be involved.

b. God wants Isaiah to respond to him with implicit trust.

1. C. S. Lewis, *The Problem of Pain* (1940; San Francisco: HarperSanFrancisco, 2001), p. 123.

c. God intends to describe the assignment, but Isaiah jumps in and volunteers before he does.

➲ If God said to you, "I want to send you on a special assignment," but didn't provide any details in advance, would you accept?

➲ Conclude your time together, if you wish, by singing or listening to a song inspired by Isaiah's experience here, such as "Here I Am, Lord" by Dan Schutte, "Burning Ember" by Steve Bell, or "Take Me In" by Kutless.

MAP OF THE ASSYRIAN EMPIRE
SHOWING LOCATIONS MENTIONED IN THE BOOK OF ISAIAH

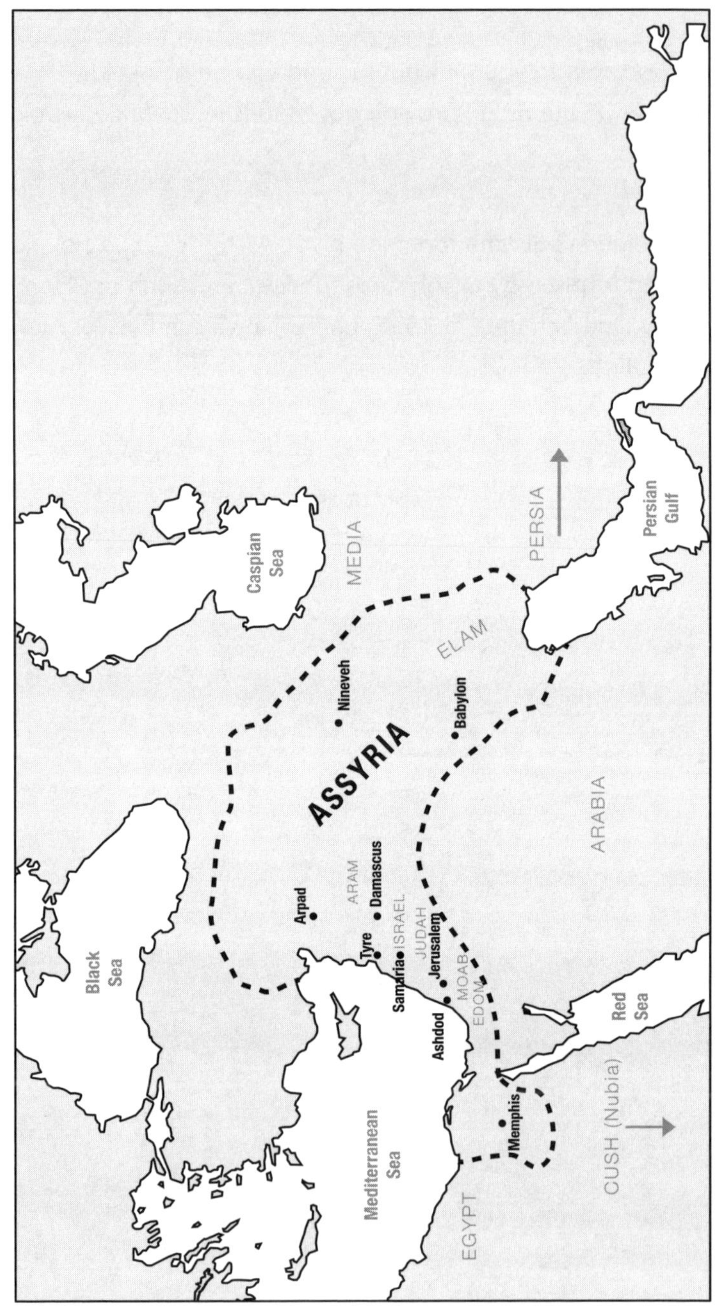

RULERS DURING ISAIAH'S TIME

Date BC	Kings of Judah	Kings of Israel	Emperors of Assyria	Pharaohs of Egypt
800				
	Uzziah (792-740)		*Assyrian empire in decline*	*Egypt divided and in decline*
		Jeroboam II (782-753)	Shalmaneser IV (782-772)	
			Assurdan III (771-754)	
		Zechariah (753) Shallum (752)	Ashur-nirari (753-746)	
750	Jotham (750-735)	Menahem (752-742)	Tiglath-pileser III (745-727) *revived empire*	Piankhy (747-716) *Nubian who began conquest of Egypt*
		Pekahiah (742-740)		
	Ahaz (735-715)	Pekah (740-732)	Shalmaneser V (727-722)	
		Hoshea (732-722) *Assyrians conquer Israel*	Sargon II (722-705)	
	Hezekiah (715-686)			Shabaka (716-702) *Nubians control all of Egypt*
700			Sennacherib (705-681) *Invaded Judah*	Shabataka (702-690)
				Tirhakah (690-664)

SESSION 3

ISAIAH DESCRIBES THE BIRTH OF CHILDREN WHO HAVE PROPHETIC NAMES AND TITLES

Book of Isaiah > Part One > Isaiah Challenges Ahaz

Note: This session is longer than usual because it develops some principles that are important for interpreting all the prophecies in the book of Isaiah. You may wish to use more than one meeting of your group to complete this session.

INTRODUCTION

Right after the passage that describes Isaiah's calling, there's a short collection of brief historical accounts that have a few prophetic oracles interspersed. (We'll learn more about what prophetic oracles are, and how they work, in the next session.) This collection provides a good illustration of how the materials in the book of Isaiah are organized. As will be explained below for each of the readings, these passages are tied together on the basis of common themes, language, and imagery. Often a phrase near the beginning of one passage echoes a similar phrase at the end of the preceding one. These are called "catch phrases."

This collection gives us the only details we have about Isaiah's personal life. But because the emphasis in its passages is on how the nation of Judah should respond to the Assyrian crisis, these details are tantalizingly few and cryptic. And so these passages present some uncertainties that interpreters have wrestled with down through the centuries.

READING

Right after the account of Isaiah's calling, which you read last time, there's a description of how Aram and Israel invaded Judah to put "the son of Tabeel" (a puppet king) on Judah's throne. You read most of this in session 1. Have someone now finish reading this account for the group, beginning where Isaiah says, "Hear now, you house of David!" and ending where he says, "he will bring the king of Assyria."

Then have different people read the remaining passages in this collection, beginning at these places:

- "In that day the LORD will whistle for flies from the Nile delta in Egypt." (This oracle is associated with the previous account by the reference to curds and honey. It explains that after enduring the depredations of the Egyptian and Assyrian empires, the country will be so depopulated that only these rudimental foods will be sustainable.)
- "The LORD said to me, 'Take a large scroll.'" (Like the first passage in the collection, this one describes how Aram and Israel will be defeated by the time a child soon to be born reaches an early stage of life. This passage repeats the term Immanuel, using it first as a name and then as a phrase, "God is with us.")
- "This is what the LORD says to me with his strong hand upon me." (This passage again contrasts the people's fear of the invasion with the faith and trust they should have in God.)
- "When someone tells you to consult mediums and spiritists." (This passage is connected to the preceding one by the references to "God's instruction" and the "testimony of warning.")
- "Nevertheless, there will be no more gloom for those who were in distress," ending with, "The zeal of the LORD Almighty will accomplish this." (The references to gloom, distress, and darkness at the beginning of this oracle match the ones at the end of the previous passage.)

DISCUSSION

1 Who is the child who will be born and named Immanuel? This is the question that has generated the greatest amount of debate among interpreters in this part of the book of Isaiah.

Ever since New Testament times, Jesus' followers have understood his birth to be a fulfillment of this prophecy. There's every reason to see it that way, as we'll discuss under the next point. But this cannot be the complete answer to the question. Isaiah's prophecy had to be meaningful in its own time, or it couldn't have been a word from God to Ahaz and the people of Judah in response to the Assyrian crisis. So the prediction must have referred initially to a child who would be born at that time, whose birth would have importance for the nation in light of the danger it was facing. Interpreters have offered many different suggestions about who this child might have been. It's not possible to summarize all of them here. Instead, we'll consider one likely explanation.

It's probable that the same child is actually being described by the two different names Immanuel and Maher-Shalal-Hash-Baz. Indeed, after describing how he named his son Maher-Shalal-Hash-Baz, Isaiah then calls this same son Immanuel in the following oracle. It was not unusual for a person in this culture to be given more than one name. This was usually the result of some important event in their life; we see this happen often as the story of the Bible unfolds. But since children's names are so significant in the passages in this collection, it's reasonable that Isaiah is using two different names for the same child to communicate two vital messages. Immanuel means "God is with us," emphasizing that the nation of Judah can trust God for protection from this invasion. Maher-Shalal-Hash-Baz means "quick to the plunder, swift to the spoil," signifying that "the wealth of Damascus and the plunder of Samaria will be carried off by the king of Assyria."

In each case Isaiah refers to the child's mother by a title rather than a name. He calls Immanuel's mother "the virgin." The Hebrew term is *almah*, signifying a young woman of marriageable age. (The English word *maiden* is similar in meaning.) Isaiah expects his listeners to know who he has in mind, since the word "the" restricts the meaning to just one person. He similarly calls the mother of Maher-Shalal-Hash-Baz "the prophetess." While the meaning of this term would include the likelihood that the woman herself had prophetic gifts, once again the word "the" suggests a particular person. In this case the likely meaning is "the woman who is married to the prophet" (Isaiah himself) or "the woman who will be married to the prophet." (When Isaiah says that he made love with this woman, he uses a specialized Hebrew expression that describes the first sexual relations between a new husband and wife.)

All of this suggests the following reconstruction of the situation. Isaiah is predicting, as a sign from God, that the woman he is about to marry will have a son. Before that son reaches an early stage of life—knowing right from wrong, beginning to speak—Aram and Israel will be defeated by Assyria. (This actually happened in the years ahead, with a series of conquests by the Assyrians. The final deportations of Israel's population took place sixty-five years later, just as Isaiah predicted to Ahaz.) The two names of this child signify that the people don't need to fear this invasion, which will soon be turned back, but they do need to trust in their God, who is with them to protect and defend them.

The only difficulty with this reconstruction is that when Isaiah first goes to speak with Ahaz, he already has a son, Shear-Jashub, who's old enough to accompany him. The mother of a boy this age would not be described as an *almah*. Some interpreters have suggested that this is actually the child of Isaiah's first wife, who has now died, and that the widowed prophet is about to remarry. This, of course, is speculative. But what we can say about this boy is that he, too, has a prophetic name. Shear-Jashub means "a remnant will return." Isaiah gave his son this hopeful name in response to what God told him six years earlier when he first called him to be a prophet: Even though the Lord would "send everyone far away" into exile, a remnant (symbolized by a tree stump) would survive to give the nation a new start. And so Isaiah says aptly, "Here am I, and the children the Lord has given me. We are signs and symbols in Israel from the Lord Almighty."

➲ What does your name mean? Do you know why your parents chose this name for you? If you have children, what names have you given them, and why? Can you see a spiritual significance in your name, even if it wasn't originally chosen with this in mind?

➲ What situation in your life is causing you the greatest fear right now? Can the assurance that God is with you enable you to respond to this situation with faith and trust and to "wait for the LORD" to help you?

➲ Isaiah describes his contemporaries turning to "mediums and spiritists" instead of to their God. If you formerly looked to sources like these for spiritual help and guidance, but have now turned instead to God, share your story with the group. (You can also tell a friend's story if they wouldn't mind.)

➲ What situations in the world today are like the one described in the second passage in this collection, where a land has been devastated and the remaining population is leading a subsistence existence? What could your group do to help in one such situation?

2 Events that occur and words that are spoken at earlier points in the unfolding story of God may come to have a fuller and deeper meaning in light of later developments in that story. When they do, these events and words are said in the Bible to be fulfilled.

Immanuel's birth is one such event. When Mary conceived Jesus without the participation of a human father, this was a far greater fulfillment of Isaiah's prophecy that an *almah* would conceive and bear a son than the one that took place in his own day. Those who lived in the time of Jesus were better able to recognize that Isaiah's words had the potential to describe such an extraordinary event because a popular translation of the Hebrew Scriptures into Greek, the common language of the time, rendered the term *almah* as *parthenos*. This Greek word describes not so much a woman who has reached marriageable age as a woman who has never had sexual relations with a man (although this was the norm for brides in the ancient Hebrew culture and so would have been implicit in the word *almah*). This translation allowed a deepening of meaning by which Isaiah's words were applied to a woman who conceived and bore a son while she was still a virgin, not by natural means after marrying a man. But perhaps the most significant deepening of meaning was that this virgin's son was literally "God with us," that is, God come to earth in human form in the person of Jesus.

Did Isaiah look ahead into the future and foresee all of this, in addition to what he foresaw regarding his own day? As we'll see in the rest of the book, Isaiah was given remarkable insights into God's plans to bring salvation to the whole world, so we should be very open to this possibility. But we should still be careful to appreciate how Isaiah's prophecies find their initial fulfillment in his own place and time, and not miss this aspect of their significance by reflecting only on their later fulfillments, as glorious as those are.

➲ Can you describe a personal experience that illustrates this concept of fulfillment, in which something you once said or did took on a deeper meaning in light of later developments in your life? (You can give group members the opportunity to reflect on this and share their answers at a later meeting.)

➲ How valuable is it for followers of Jesus today to understand the meaning of Isaiah's prophecies for his own contemporaries, and not just recognize that many of them find a deeper fulfillment in the life of Jesus? Put another way, if we already know how the story of God culminates, what is the value of knowing earlier parts of the story?

3 The child described in the last oracle in this collection is probably not the son of Isaiah. While many scholars believe that Isaiah was of royal blood, since he appears to have been a member of the court who had access to Judah's kings, his descendants were not in line for the throne. But this child is a future king who will "reign on David's throne and over his kingdom." And so many interpreters believe this oracle is describing the crown prince Hezekiah, the eldest son of Ahaz, who was about six years old at this time.

The emphasis in this oracle is that the fortunes of the nation will be revived under this next king. Judah did indeed prosper under Hezekiah, who eliminated idol worship, repaired the temple, restored respect for God's law, strengthened the nation militarily, and pushed back its enemies. But the most important message of this oracle is that Judah's next king will not be the "son of Tabeel," the man the invading armies want to set up as their puppet in the land. Judah already has a rightful heir—"to us a son is given"—and God will preserve the throne of David so that this heir can take his proper place upon it. Once more a child symbolizes God's intention to protect and preserve the people from these invaders—if they will only depend on him.

These prophecies, too, have a later fulfillment in the life of Jesus. The areas described here as in distress and darkness were the first parts of the kingdom of Israel to be overrun by the Assyrians. In the New Testament, the promise that the people living in these areas would see a great light is applied to the fact that Jesus began his public ministry there. And while the child's amazing titles—Wonderful Counselor, Mighty God, Everlasting Father, Prince of Peace—could indicate in the original context how the king represented God as the nation's ruler, followers of Jesus see in these titles a description of who he actually was: the earthly incarnation of God.

The people of Israel and Judah were expecting God to send them a supreme deliverer called the Messiah, meaning the "anointed one" (that is, the chosen one). Whenever prophecies, in addition to their original meaning, can be understood to look forward to this figure, they are known as *Messianic prophecies*. In this session we've already seen two of them (about Immanuel and about this future king), and we'll see many more in the rest of the book.

➲ Which of these titles is most meaningful to you as a description of Jesus? Why?

- Wonderful Counselor
- Mighty God
- Everlasting Father
- Prince of Peace

➲ Conclude your time together, if you wish, by singing or listening to a song such as "Immanuel (A Sign Shall Be Given)" by Michael Card, or by watching an internet video of a performance of the chorus "For Unto Us a Child Is Born" from Handel's *Messiah*.

SESSION 4

GOD ACCUSES ISRAEL AND JUDAH OF INJUSTICE AND OPPRESSION

Book of Isaiah > Part One > Opening Oracles

INTRODUCTION

Now that we've learned what we can about Isaiah personally, it's time to go back to the start of the book and consider the messages he brought from God during the Assyrian crisis. All of the oracles collected in Part One relate to this crisis. But they're not in chronological order. Some of the ones you'll consider in this session come from a time when the nation was being devastated by invaders, but these could come either from the reign of Ahaz, when Aram and Israel invaded Judah, or from the reign of Hezekiah, when the Assyrians invaded. These oracles are actually sequenced on the basis of similarities in their language, themes, and imagery, just like the ones we considered in session 3.

Prophetic oracles are poems or songs that are often based on one or more extended images. For example, in the last session you saw how Isaiah used the images of a stream and a river to describe how the Assyrians would overwhelm the land ("the mighty floodwaters of the Euphrates" would "sweep on into Judah"). Prophets sometimes develop their images in surprising ways. In the last session you also saw the Assyrians described as a swarm of bees, but the people were then depicted as eating honey. Prophetic oracles may also use wordplay to bring their point home. Finally, some oracles, like the third one you'll read in this session, are based on the repetition of an idea rather than the development of an image.

The overall theme of the oracles collected in Part One of Isaiah is ruin and restoration: God will punish and correct the nation through its reverses and misfortunes, but then restore and rebuild it. The theme of restoration is emphasized by its placement in the center of the collection. In most writing today, the important points are made at the beginning and the end, but the Hebrews tended to put them in the middle.

The word *prophecy* can describe both foretelling (predicting the future) and forth-telling, denouncing injustice. Much more of the book of Isaiah, and the other prophetic books in the Bible, is forth-telling rather than foretelling.

READING

Have different people take turns reading the oracles at the start of Part One of the book of Isaiah, beginning at these places:

- "Hear me, you heavens! Listen, earth!" This oracle uses the image of domesticated animals to illustrate how little sense the Israelites must have to disregard their Lord and Master.
- "Woe to the sinful nation, a people whose guilt is great." This oracle is connected to the previous one through the shared image of disobedient children. But its sustained image is that of an individual soldier badly beaten and wounded in battle, who represents the devastated state of the countryside under invasion.
- "Hear the word of the Lord, you rulers of Sodom; listen to the instruction of our God, you people of Gomorrah!" This oracle is a litany rather than a sustained image: it's built on the repeated idea that God does not want insincere worship in any form, and so it presents a long list of forms of worship.
- "'Come now, let us settle the matter,' says the Lord." This oracle describes sins as scarlet and red, evoking the way the previous one said the people's hands were full of blood. The sustained idea in this oracle is that of transformation. There's wordplay here as well: in Hebrew blood is *dam* and red is

adam. Isaiah also gives the people the choice of *eating* the best in the land or *being eaten* ("devoured") by the sword. His propensity for this kind of wordplay is another reason why scholars consider him to have been an educated member of the court.
- "See how the faithful city has become a prostitute!" This oracle shares the theme of transformation with the preceding oracle. In this case, the city that has been transformed from good to bad will be transformed back again, so that it will be faithful and righteous once more. But those who forsake the LORD will change from verdant to dry and ultimately burn up.
- "This is what Isaiah son of Amoz saw concerning Judah and Jerusalem" (ending "Come, descendants of Jacob, let us walk in the light of the LORD"). This oracle echoes and responds to the themes of many of the earlier ones. For example, the sword no longer devours, but provides food; the nations now come to Jerusalem not as invaders but as worshippers of the God of Jacob. This central oracle about restoration is so important that it bears a special heading referring again to Isaiah.

DISCUSSION

1 An overall theme runs through these opening oracles in the book: God has a dispute with the people of Israel. At one point the LORD, speaking through Isaiah, even employs legal terminology. When he says, "Come now, let us settle the matter," he's using the term for a court case between two parties. (It's the same term that Isaiah uses when he says that God will "settle disputes" between peoples.)

This explains why the book doesn't use the life of Isaiah as its organizing principle and present his sayings and the events of his life in chronological order. It's not a biography. It's a legal case, against the two houses of Israel for breaking their covenant with the LORD. As such, it opens with a formal accusation against them. They have rebelled, and this is why they are suffering.

When Isaiah invokes the heavens and the earth as witnesses against Israel, he's alluding to the way Moses told the people, as recorded in the book of Deuteronomy, that he would "call the heavens and the earth to testify against them" if they broke the covenant. Moses then summoned these witnesses by saying, "Listen, you heavens . . . hear, you earth." Isaiah is making a direct allusion to this saying in the oracle that has been placed at the head of this book to open the case against the covenant-breaking nation.

➲ To get a sense for the force that Isaiah's words would have had in his day, reword the third oracle in contemporary language. Think of places and people that have become synonymous with evil and call your own country and its leaders by their names. Then substitute as many different contemporary worship practices as you can for the ancient ones listed in this oracle. (For example, "'The multitude of your praise songs—what are they to me?' says the LORD.") When you get to the part of the oracle that describes how the people should be practicing justice, use present-day examples. Does this give you a sense of how horrific these words would have sounded to the people?

2 What are the specific charges against Israel? They've broken the covenant in one way by worshipping other gods and spirits. You saw last time how they were consulting mediums and spiritists, and you've seen this time how they were frequenting oak groves and gardens, places where pagan deities were honored. But this is not God's main complaint against them.

Instead, God is enraged by the injustice and oppression that have filled the nation now that the protections for the poor and defenseless built into the law of Moses are being ignored. He swears that he will purge the wicked oppressors from the nation and make it a place of justice and righteousness again.

➲ Who in our world corresponds with the orphans and widows who were defenseless and exploited in Isaiah's time? What kinds of things are happening to these people today?

➲ If you're aware of things that followers of Jesus are doing to improve these people's situations, mention these to the group. Give people the opportunity to describe how they're personally supporting efforts like these.

➲ Isaiah characterizes his own society as highly unjust and immoral by comparing it to Sodom and Gomorrah. Where would you put your own society on a scale from extremely just and moral to extremely unjust and immoral? Why?

3 Another thing that's infuriating God is the way the people are maintaining the outward forms of their worship—sacrifices and festivals—even though they're guilty of injustice and oppression. God says he'd rather have no worship at all than insincere worship like this. "When you spread out your hands in prayer, I hide my eyes," he says, because "your hands are full of blood!" But God will discipline and purify the people so that Jerusalem will be a place where all nations can come and learn God's ways, and then the entire world will be transformed into a place of peace and justice.

➲ Why are people who are guilty of great injustices sometimes also quite religious, without responding to their own religion's message about the need for confession and repentance? What do they think is in it for them if they worship God outwardly without making any change on the inside?

➲ What do you picture when you imagine a world without war? In what ways would such a world be different from the one we know today? Once again, if you're aware of things that followers of Jesus are doing to promote world peace, as an expression of their commitment to the kind of world God wants to bring about one day, tell the group about their efforts. How could you support them?

SESSION 5

ISRAEL AND JUDAH ARE FOUND GUILTY OF INJUSTICE AND OPPRESSION

Book of Isaiah > Part One > Opening Oracles, Continued

INTRODUCTION

In this session you'll continue reading the oracles in Part One of the book of Isaiah. The last oracle you read in session 4 offered a brief respite. It envisioned the glorious restoration of Jerusalem. But now God continues to make the case against Israel through his prophet. Forth-telling continues as judgment is threatened against the nation for its idolatry, greed, and injustice—all things that violate its covenant with the Lord. Isaiah uses legal language again when he says that God "takes his place in court" and "enters into judgment against the elders and leaders of his people." The case culminates when God tells a story about a vineyard that was carefully cultivated but still produced wild grapes and then asks the people of Judah and Jerusalem to "judge between me and my vineyard." The judgment any impartial person would give—that the vineyard deserves to become "a wasteland, neither pruned nor cultivated"—is then pronounced against the disobedient nation as a whole.

Several of the oracles you'll read in this session appear to have been delivered early in Isaiah's career as a prophet, some years before the ones you read last time. They describe the prosperity and security that the nation was still enjoying in the wake of Uzziah's long reign in the few years after his death. But they also warn that things are about to change drastically. All of the things that have made the nation think it can find security apart from God—military might, material prosperity, and idolatrous religion—will soon be stripped away from it. Indeed, there are indications in some of these oracles that this has already begun to happen ("Jerusalem staggers, Judah is falling"). There's only a brief mention of restoration in a short oracle about the renewed glory of Jerusalem. It comes just before the case against Israel is concluded with a resounding verdict of guilty.

READING

Begin your reading where you left off in session 4. Have different people take turns reading the oracles that start at the following places:

- "You, Lord, have abandoned your people, the descendants of Jacob."
- "The Lord Almighty has a day in store for all the proud and lofty."
- "See now, the Lord, the Lord Almighty, is about to take from Jerusalem and Judah both supply and support."
- "Jerusalem staggers, Judah is falling."
- "The Lord says, 'The women of Zion are haughty.'"
- "In that day the Branch of the Lord will be beautiful and glorious."
- "I will sing for the one I love a song about his vineyard" (ending, "And he looked for justice, but saw bloodshed; for righteousness, but heard cries of distress").

As you listen to these oracles, notice how they work. Most of them are litanies that drive their point home through repetition. However, the last oracle is based instead on an image from the natural world that's developed and then applied to the human world. This last oracle is identified as a song. The second one you'll read may also have been sung, since near its end it has a repeated chorus:

> From the fearful presence of the Lord
> and the splendor of his majesty,
> when he rises to shake the earth.

(This chorus echoes the ending of the first oracle.)

DISCUSSION

1 The oracle about the glorious restoration of Jerusalem (session 4) says that God will exalt that city, once it is purified, to make it a source of truth and justice for the whole world. By contrast, Isaiah now says that God will humble all those who exalt themselves, who take pride in their wealth, might, and idols. When God appears in his glory, people will hide in holes and caverns and throw their idols to the moles and bats who live there. This may be a reference to an impending divine judgment that will demonstrate how powerless these idols are to save anyone. Isaiah predicts that the people's governmental, military, and religious leaders, along with their skilled artisans—all sources of national pride—will soon be taken away, leaving only the poor and inexperienced as potential leaders. This actually happened in the northern kingdom of Israel less than twenty years after Uzziah died, when the Assyrians overran that country and carried off all of its elites into exile.

➲ What kinds of things do people in your society take pride in? What do they treat as means by which they can get ahead in life, without depending on God or becoming interdependent with other people? If you've ever seen a person (including yourself) go through an experience that made them realize they needed to depend on God rather than things like these, tell the group about this experience.

➲ Isaiah urges God not to forgive the Israelites for their pride, idolatry, and oppression. He asks him to punish and humble them instead. Why do you think Isaiah prayed like this? Do you think that a person could do something so wicked and evil that they shouldn't be rescued from its consequences in this life, even if they recognize their wrong and ask God for forgiveness, but instead should be punished openly as a warning to others, and so satisfy the demands of justice?

2 Isaiah speaks an oracle against the wealthy women of Jerusalem, who are far more concerned with enhancing their appearance through fashion and cosmetics than with having an influence for justice in their land. Isaiah says that all of their finery will be stripped away, just as the nation's sources of defiant pride will be taken from it. (Indeed, as the oracle's message is transferred from individuals to the community, Zion herself, personified as a woman, sits desolately on the ground.) The prophet says at the end of this oracle that the nation's wars will kill so many of its male soldiers that seven women will approach one surviving man and ask only to be given his name as their husband, without any support, so that they can at least have some semblance of the status that marriage confers in this society. This parallels the ending of the third oracle you read for this session, in which a clan desperate for leadership turns to one of their members who at least still owns a cloak—only to find that he, too, is actually destitute. These oracles illustrate that when people depend on their own resources in defiance of God, they're eventually reduced to depending on whatever they can find.

➲ Many of the fashion items that Isaiah lists are particular to his cultural context, such as nose rings, jingling ankle bracelets, veils, headbands, and sashes. If your culture is significantly different, what would some of its equivalents be? That is, what items, especially if many were worn all at once, would represent ostentatious consumption?

➲ In your society, are women treated with greater deference and accorded higher status if they use cosmetics and wear the latest fashions? Do men get similar advantages from cultivating their appearance? How much money, time, and attention can a follower of Jesus responsibly devote to looking good?

3 Throughout all of his oracles Isaiah makes ingenious use of literary techniques, in ways too numerous to mention. Some of his artistry is nearly impossible to convey in a translation, such as the wordplay involved when Isaiah calls idols not *elim* (gods) but *elilim* (worthless things), or when God says in the song of the vineyard that he looked for justice (*mishpat*) but saw bloodshed (*mishpach*), and for righteousness (*tsedaqah*) but heard cries of distress (*tse'aqah*). However, it is still possible to catch much of Isaiah's literary brilliance, such as the irony involved when people who want to bow down (to their idols) get what they want and are brought low in humiliation. Sometimes suitable English words are available to translate his similar-sounding Hebrew terms (for example, "supply" and "support" for *mash'en* and *mash'enah*). But the prophet's powerful command of language and his literary artistry are probably felt most keenly in those places where he develops a vivid image and then strikingly brings it home by applying it directly to his hearers. For example, he portrays an owner cultivating a vineyard and waiting expectantly for good fruit, then reveals that the LORD has cultivated Israel and has been waiting for justice to appear, only to be deeply disappointed.

➲ What do you think of the idea that God has put in place all of the influences necessary for your life, and for the life of your community, to produce justice and righteousness, so that God can expectantly wait for these things? What might some of these influences be? Where is God finding good fruit? Where is there still bad fruit?

GOD PASSES SENTENCE AGAINST ISRAEL AND JUDAH

Book of Isaiah > Part One > Seven Woes

INTRODUCTION

Once a guilty verdict has been declared against Israel and Judah, the sentencing follows. This takes the form of a complex oracle that pronounces seven woes against the disobedient nation. These woes enumerate the crimes of which it has been convicted, which express its failure to produce the justice and righteousness that God is looking for. The woes are punctuated at several points by descriptions of the punishments the people will suffer (these are typically introduced by "therefore").

After the sixth woe, a new voice warns that even these punishments will not satisfy the demands of justice: "Yet for all this, his anger is not turned away, his hand is still upraised." This indicates that the destruction Aram and Israel have caused by their invasion of Judah does not represent the full punishment needed for the nation's idolatry, greed, and oppression. (Indeed, the people's pride has been unaffected by the recent devastation of their land. They are already saying, now that this first invasion is over, "The bricks have fallen down, but we will rebuild with dressed stone; the fig trees have been felled, but we will replace them with cedars.")

The oracle then depicts the impending further judgments in more detail, with the refrain repeated three more times: "Yet for all this, his anger is not turned away . . ." Finally the seventh woe is announced, with one more description of judgment and a final echo of the refrain. These interlocking sequences of repetition shape this oracle into a complex litany. Overall, it follows a favored pattern of Hebrew composition: it presents a series of six things and then, after some suspenseful heightening, it introduces a seventh.

The accounts of Isaiah's calling and personal life that you considered in sessions 2 and 3 have actually been inserted right in the middle of this complex oracle. (You will need to skip over them as you read through it.) This is probably intended to illustrate how Isaiah's "testimony of warning" was "sealed up" for his disciples and for future generations when his counsel to Ahaz was rejected. The placement of these accounts within this oracle is determined by a catch phrase. They're inserted right at the point where the oracle says, "If one looks at the land (*erets*), there is only darkness and distress"; this corresponds with a similar statement near the end of the accounts, "Then they will look toward the earth (*erets*) and see only distress and darkness."

READING

Assign four people to read the different components of this complex oracle, taking these parts:

A. The voice of woe, pronouncing the woes
B. The voice of sentencing, announcing the punishments
C. The voice of warning, declaring that justice is not yet satisfied
D. The voice of doom, describing future judgments

The parts begin at these places:

A. "Woe to you who add house to house"

  B. "The Lord Almighty has declared in my hearing"

A. "Woe to those who rise early in the morning to run after their drinks"

  B. "Therefore my people will go into exile"

  B. "Therefore Death expands its jaws"

A. "Woe to those who draw sin along with cords of deceit"

A. "Woe to those who call evil good and good evil"

A. "Woe to those who are wise in their own eyes"

A. "Woe to those who are heroes at drinking wine"

B. "Therefore, as tongues of fire lick up straw"

B. "Therefore the LORD's anger burns against his people"

C. "Yet for all this, his anger is not turned away"

D. "He lifts up a banner for the distant nations"

skip over the material you considered in sessions 2 and 3

D. "The LORD has sent a message against Jacob"

C. "Yet for all this, his anger is not turned away"

D. "But the people have not returned to him who struck them"

C. "Yet for all this, his anger is not turned away"

D. "Surely wickedness burns like a fire"

C. "Yet for all this, his anger is not turned away"

A. "Woe to those who make unjust laws"

B. "What will you do on the day of reckoning?"

C. "Yet for all this, his anger is not turned away, his hand is still upraised."

DISCUSSION

➲ The book of Isaiah clearly has a complex structure that's unlike just about any work that would be composed today. Have you seen people do any of the following in response to this complexity?

a. Just plow through the book chapter by chapter figuring that's got to be good for them somehow.

b. Leave Isaiah to the experts and read something else in the Bible.

c. Equip themselves to appreciate its ancient form by drawing on informative resources and read in community so that everyone can help each other.

➲ Look back over each of the seven woes and describe who the people named would correspond to in your society. For example, who today would "add house to house and join field to field" until they "live alone in the land," that is, buy up many small lots, destroying the supply of affordable housing, and build a mansion for themselves with no neighbors? Does the community of Jesus' followers today have a prophetic calling, like Isaiah's in his own time, to warn that God opposes actions like these?

➲ Isaiah says that when God punishes the nation for its oppression, greed, and debauchery, "the holy God will be *proved holy* by his righteous acts." What do you think he means by this?

PART ONE IN DETAIL:

(session numbers)

(4) Accustion against Israel & Judah

(5) Verdict against Israel & Judah

(6) Sentence against Israel & Judah

(2) Isaiah's call

(3) Isaiah challenges Ahaz

(6) Sentence against Israel & Judah

(12) Resolution of Assyrian crisis

THE BOOK OF ISAIAH AND THE ASSYRIAN CRISIS

Passages in Isaiah (Session #)	**Dates BC**	**World Events**
Opening oracles of Part One (4-6)	734-701	Assyrian crisis as a whole
God calls Isaiah to be a prophet (2)	740	King Uzziah of Judah dies
Isaiah challenges Ahaz (3)	734	Aram and Israel invade Judah
Prophecy against Damascus (7) Original prophecy against Moab (8)	732	Assyrians defeat rebel coalition, destroy Damascus
First woe against Judah (7)	722	Assyrians destroy Samaria
Prophecy against land of whirring wings (8) Prophecy against Philistines (8) Prophecy against Moab updated (8)	715	Nubians achieve control of Egypt, encourage rebellion against Assyria
Prophecy against Egypt (9)	711	Assyrians crush revolt, Egyptians surrender Yamani of Ashdod
Third woe against Judah (9)	710-701	Judah cultivates Egyptian alliance
Prophecies against Desert by the Sea, Dumah, Arabia (10)	705	Sargon killed in battle, uprisings in east and west
Fourth and fifth woes against Judah (10) Prophecy against Tyre (10)	703-701	Sennacherib defeats eastern coalition, brings army against western rebels
Narrative of Hezekiah's illness (13)	703	Babylonian envoys visit Hezekiah
Prophecy against the Valley of Vision (11)	701	Sennacherib defeats Egyptians, threatens Jerusalem
Narrative of Surrender Demand (11) Second and sixth woes (11) Closing oracles of Part One (12)	701	Sennacherib's army destroyed by the angel of the LORD

Note: Scholars differ as to exactly what events are being addressed in various passages; this chart represents widely held understandings.

SESSION 7

THE REVOLT AGAINST ASSYRIA IN 734–732 BC

Book of Isaiah > Part Two: Prophecies Against the Nations > Damascus
Book of Isaiah > Part Four: Woes Against Judah > First Woe

INTRODUCTION

So far we've considered most of the oracles and stories in Part One of the book of Isaiah. They depict how Judah struggled against the Assyrian empire's encroachment throughout Isaiah's lifetime. The prophecies against the nations in Part Two and the woes in Part Four provide more information about this Assyrian crisis. (Part Three relates to a later time period.)

In the next several sessions (7–11) we'll consider these prophecies and woes in detail. This will enable us to view the crisis from an international perspective. We'll see how Judah's leaders were often tempted to rely on military alliances rather than God's protection. When we get to session 11 we'll also read the story in Part Six of how Assyria invaded Judah and discover how the crisis was resolved. Then in session 12 we'll return to Part One and consider its closing oracles, which offer hope for the future to the Judeans who have survived the Assyrian invasion.

To help locate the prophecies and woes we'll be discussing, you can look back at the summaries of Parts Two and Four in session 1 (pages 14-15 and 16). You can find the different nations that are mentioned on the map on page 24. The chart on page 47 shows how these prophecies and woes line up with international developments.

We'll begin in this session with the prophecies and woes that come from the beginning of the crisis in 734 BC when Aram and Israel invaded Judah. (You read the story of this invasion in session 3.)

READING AND DISCUSSION

1 Have someone read the prophecy against Damascus out loud for the group. (It's the fifth one in Part Two. You should have highlighted or marked its opening line when you skimmed through the book in session 1. It begins, "A prophecy [or "oracle" or "burden"] against Damascus.")

Isaiah's prophecies against the nations demonstrate a familiarity with international developments; this is one more reason why interpreters believe he was a member of the royal court. He delivered this oracle around 734 BC, as Judah was being invaded by Aram and Israel. (He speaks of "many nations that rage," likely including their allies against Assyria: the Philistines, Moab, and Edom.) The armies assembled against Judah are such a deadly threat that their approach seems like the "roar of surging waters." Nevertheless, Isaiah predicts that Damascus, the capital of Aram, will be destroyed and that both Aram and Israel will ultimately be devastated and deserted. These words began to be fulfilled within two years, when the Assyrian armies came and subdued the rebellious nations, besieging and destroying Damascus.

The customary pattern in Isaiah's oracles is to move from a symbolic depiction in the natural world to the actual situation in the human world. This prophecy reverses that pattern. After describing the destruction of Damascus more literally, it uses harvest imagery to illustrate that Israel will be left with only a few survivors. Isaiah then explains the reason for God's judgment against Israel: the people have turned away from him to worship the idols of the Canaanites. As a result, in an ironic judgment, their cities will be abandoned, just as the Canaanites abandoned their own strongholds when the Israelites displaced them. The oracle then promises that God will deliver Judah from this invasion and concludes with the observation, equally ironic, that the only "portion" the would-be looters will actually obtain is terror and destruction.

➲ Isaiah tells the people living in the northern kingdom of Israel, "You have forgotten God your Savior." They have a long, rich heritage of faith, but they have now turned to worship the gods of the Canaanites—even though these gods have already been proven powerless. What causes societies that were once shaped by biblical principles to start following contrary influences instead? Is this an inevitable trend? Or can it be reversed once it has started? If so, how?

➲ Do you know a person who appears to have forgotten God their Savior? Without naming any names, describe for the group how this person once followed God and what you think led them into a life that is now directed by other influences. Isaiah promises in this prophecy that a remnant will turn back to the "Holy One of Israel." Have you ever seen someone apparently abandon God but then return? If so, tell their story.

2 The first woe in Part Four of the book of Isaiah (which begins, "Woe to that wreath, the pride of Ephraim's drunkards") was composed a few years after the prophecy against Damascus. It starts by addressing the people of the northern kingdom of Israel, but then, about halfway through, it turns to address the people of the southern kingdom of Judah. Have people take turns reading through this oracle one stanza at a time, ending with, "All this also comes from the Lord Almighty, whose plan is wonderful, whose wisdom is magnificent." (In most Bibles the stanzas will be separated by a little extra white space. If they aren't in your edition, change readers whenever you come to what seems like a natural transition.)

This oracle was delivered in the few years after the destruction of Damascus in 732 BC. It declares that Samaria, the capital of Israel, will soon be destroyed as well. Samaria was popularly described as a wreath or garland because its walls encircled the hill on which it was built. But Isaiah uses this image instead to describe the debauchery of the city. He paints a picture of drunken partygoers putting on wreaths that end up being trampled in the mud by the end of the night. But like most of Isaiah's prophecies, this one envisions restoration as well as ruin: He says that the Lord Almighty will one day be a beautiful wreath for the remnant of his people. However, he then returns to present-day conditions and describes them in graphic terms, depicting how the political and religious leaders are perpetually drunk, so that the nation has no wise guidance and is heading for destruction.

In this oracle we can hear Israel's leaders complain that Isaiah is speaking to them as if they are children who need to be told the basics of right and wrong: "Do this, do that." (Even though Isaiah lived in Judah, his words clearly had an impact on the surrounding nations.) These leaders are interpreting his calls for justice as an appeal to simplistic rules that are beneath sophisticated people like themselves. But their supposed sophistry is really just rationalization for doing wrong. And so, the prophet says, God will have to speak to them through a foreign power that will conquer them and order them around as prisoners: "Do this, do that."

Once again Isaiah's predictions came true. When Israel launched a fresh revolt against the Assyrians, they returned and destroyed Samaria in 722 BC, devastating the country and deporting much of its population.

➲ Have you ever had an experience where you had to go back to the basics and learn something the hard way? If so, share it with the group. Did you see God at work in the situation? How?

➲ Does any reliable moral system need to begin with basic statements of right and wrong (such as the Ten Commandments), which can then be interpreted and applied to address more complicated, ambiguous situations? Or has a postmodern world moved past this kind of "foundationalism," so that moral systems now need a different basis? If so, what would that be?

3 After depicting the fate of Israel, Isaiah turns to address Judah. The rulers in Jerusalem are boasting that they have "entered into a covenant with death," meaning that they have somehow gotten death to agree to spare them in these perilous times. They may be speaking only figuratively, boasting of the strategy they think will preserve them. But they may also be describing how they have actually begun worshipping and serving Mot, the Canaanite god of death. Either way, their covenant is supposed to be with the LORD instead, and it's supposed to ensure justice within the nation. Isaiah predicts that God will correct the errant Judeans, using the Assyrians as a scourge, but will then demonstrate his power to deliver them. This will happen in the years ahead as the Assyrian crisis reaches a climax.

The oracle ends with an analogy drawn from the agricultural world. Isaiah describes how, if there's ever to be a harvest, plowing must be followed by planting and each different crop must be sown, threshed (grain and husk separated), and ground appropriately. He describes this as the "right way" of farming, using the same term (*mishpat*) that's used throughout the book to describe justice. This analogy illustrates how a society needs to follow the "right way" that God teaches. Rather than making a covenant with death to try to escape the consequences of turning from this way, the people of Judah must once again worship and obey the Lord Almighty, acknowledging that his "wisdom is magnificent."

➲ Isaiah uses a popular proverb of his day to describe the inadequacy of the nation's covenant with death. He says, "The bed is too short to stretch out on, the blanket too narrow to wrap around you." A Texan might express the same thought today by saying, "That dog won't hunt." Think of something a person in your society might depend on rather than God for guidance, protection, and provision. Then describe it by using a popular saying from your culture that illustrates how something falls short of its intended effect or desired purpose.

➲ What do you consider your basic trade or craft? What are some of the essential principles a person needs to follow in order to get good results? What are some of the ill-advised shortcuts people try to take, instead of following proven principles? Drawing on this analogy, what would you say are some of the elements of the "right way" a person needs to follow in life, and what are some of the shortcuts to be avoided?

SESSION 8

THE REVOLT AGAINST ASSYRIA IN 714–711 BC

Book of Isaiah > Part Two: Prophecies Against the Nations > Moab; The Philistines; The "Land of Whirring Wings"

INTRODUCTION

In this session we'll look at three more of the prophecies against the nations in Part Two of the book of Isaiah. We'll see how the kingdom of Judah came under increasing pressure to abandon its dependence on Assyria for protection and cultivate an alliance with Egypt. When it made this shift, this ultimately provoked an Assyrian invasion.

READING AND DISCUSSION

1 Have someone read the prophecy against Moab. It's the one just before the prophecy against Damascus, which you looked at last time. This oracle dates to around 732 BC. Moab was a partner with Aram and Israel in their revolt and so it, too, was invaded and punished by the Assyrian armies. This prophecy depicts all of the major settlements in the country being destroyed and abandoned, sending a stream of refugees fleeing to the south. The oracle seems to have been composed specifically in response to a request from these Moabite refugees for sanctuary within the kingdom of Judah, even though the two countries had just been enemies.

The prophet is filled with compassion for these refugees: "My heart cries out over Moab; her fugitives flee as far as Zoar." He envisions them finding shelter in Judah under a godly king from the house of David "who in judging seeks justice and speeds the cause of righteousness." Isaiah then offers a sympathetic lament for the ruined country, using one of his characteristic harvest images. ("The rulers of the nations have trampled down the choicest vines.")

It's unknown how King Ahaz actually responded to the Moabite refugees' plea for sanctuary. It is to be hoped that he granted it, since this appeal could have led to an early fulfillment of Isaiah's prophecy that all nations would look to Mount Zion and learn about justice.

➲ Have you ever helped resettle refugees in your community? If so, tell the group a little about your experience. How did you get involved? What practical needs do refugees have? What challenges do they face in adapting to a new society? In what ways are they able to preserve some of their own culture? How did the refugees you helped enrich your life?

➲ What is your country's policy on accepting refugees? (If you aren't sure, find out.) Does this policy reflect the kind of justice and righteousness that Isaiah hopes the king will show in his day? If not, are followers of Jesus in your country working to change its policy? How could you support their efforts?

2 Next, have someone read the prophecy against the Philistines, which comes just before the one against Moab. (These prophecies are out of sequence historically but are connected by catch phrases. The reference to the Philistines wailing over ruined cities connects with a description of the Moabites doing the same thing.)

This oracle is dated "in the year King Ahaz died," that is, 715 BC. It, too, is composed in response to a request from the people of another nation. The Philistines, like the Moabites, had been partners with Aram and Israel. It appears that after Assyria defeated those two nations, King Ahaz struck back against the Philistines. But now he is dead, and they have sent envoys to try to persuade the new king, Hezekiah, to join them in another coalition against the Assyrians. Isaiah responds that the LORD will protect his own people, so they don't need alliances with other nations. He adds that the Philistines shouldn't feel relief over the death of Ahaz; what he did to them was nothing compared with what the Assyrians will do in response to their current revolt. They will descend on them from the north like a "cloud of smoke," leaving burning cities in their wake.

(The prophecy against Moab ends with a footnote, probably added around the time this oracle against the Philistines was composed, which predicts that Moab will be devastated again "within three years." Moab joined the Philistines in this revolt against Assyria, which began in 714 BC. Both nations were crushed by the emperor Sargon in the year 711.)

➲ Why do you think the Philistines expected the Judeans even to consider an alliance with them when they had been enemies so recently? Did they expect them to sense the growing danger of Assyria and calculate that "the enemy of my enemy is my friend"? Have you ever been in a situation where you were tempted to join forces with a former enemy against a new opponent? How do you think God feels generally about this type of strategy?

3 Finally, have someone read the prophecy that begins "Woe to the land of whirring wings," which comes right after the prophecy against Damascus.

This is one more oracle in which Isaiah responds to an overture that another nation is making to Judah. Its details are somewhat cryptic, and interpreters differ in their understandings, but one likely explanation is as follows. Around the time Ahaz died and was succeeded by Hezekiah, the Egyptians also had a change of rulers. A new dynasty began that was Nubian, meaning that the ruling family came from the area south of Egypt that was then known as Cush, now part of Ethiopia. ("Whirring wings" may be a reference to the loud insects of that region.) At this time the Egyptian empire, newly reunified, was trying to stir up the smaller nations that provided a buffer between itself and Assyria. So long as the Assyrians had their hands full putting down rebellious coalitions of those nations, they would leave Egypt alone. It may be that the new rulers of Egypt actually incited the revolt that began in 714 BC by sending their envoys to the countries that participated. In that case the "messengers" described in this prophecy would be Egyptian envoys sent to Judah.

Judah did not join in revolt at this time, perhaps in part because of Isaiah's influence. In this oracle, the prophet tells these envoys to keep going—all the way to Assyria, the "aggressive nation of strange speech, whose land is divided by rivers"—since that's who the Egyptians are really trying to deal with. Isaiah goes on to explain that the Assyrians themselves will be subdued when the LORD eventually acts against them, and they will bring tribute to "Mount Zion, the place of the Name of the LORD Almighty."

Isaiah discerned that the Egyptian empire simply wanted to use smaller nations as pawns in its contest with Assyria. Unfortunately, many in the Judean royal court, ultimately including King Hezekiah himself, began to think they could rely on Egypt to protect them against Assyria. We'll see in the sessions ahead how this led the Assyrian crisis to a desperate and perilous climax.

➲ Whatever responses Judah's royal court may have offered to overtures like these, Isaiah responds to each of them on behalf of God. This is one important aspect of prophecy as forth-telling: speaking truth to power. Does your community of Jesus' followers use statements, policy papers, petitions, etc., to call on those in power to follow biblical principles in responding to contemporary issues? If so, describe some recent situations that have been addressed. If not, would you like to see your community, or its leaders, do this kind of thing? What issues would you like them to take up?

JUDAH MOVES FROM DEPENDENCE ON ASSYRIA TO ALLIANCE WITH EGYPT

Book of Isaiah > Part Two: Prophecies Against the Nations > Egypt
Book of Isaiah > Part Four: Woes Against Judah > Third Woe

INTRODUCTION

Even though the Assyrians consistently crushed any revolts that were launched in the region, the nations around Judah continued to scheme against their overlords as the eighth century BC drew to a close. This rebellious spirit was fueled by the Egyptians, who promised protection and support to the smaller countries that lay between them and the rival empire. Eventually even Judah began to be swayed from its allegiance to Assyria and, more importantly, from trusting in the Lord, as Isaiah was urging them to do.

Isaiah cautioned the nation and its leaders repeatedly against cultivating any alliance with the Egyptians. In this session you'll hear the case he made against such a course in his prophecy against Egypt. You'll also see how, despite his words, the Judean royal court secretly began to pursue the very policy that Isaiah warned them against.

READING AND DISCUSSION

1 Have five people read Isaiah's prophecy against Egypt. (It's in Part Two, and it comes right after the prophecy against the "land of whirring wings.") Have the readers begin at these places:

- "See, the LORD rides on a swift cloud and is coming to Egypt."
- "The waters of the river will dry up, and the riverbed will be parched and dry."
- "The officials of Zoan are nothing but fools."
- "In that day the Egyptians will become weaklings."
- "In the year that the supreme commander, sent by Sargon king of Assyria, came to Ashdod and attacked and captured it" (ending, "How then can we escape?").

In the first three parts of this oracle, Isaiah gives compelling reasons why Judah should not depend on Egypt for support and protection against the Assyrians:

a. Egypt has been racked by internal divisions and civil wars. This has weakened the formerly great empire to the point where the Nubians have been able to take control of it. (When Isaiah refers to a "cruel master" and "fierce king," he's probably describing the Nubian king Shabaka, who became ruler over all of Egypt around this time, 714 BC.) Why, Isaiah asks, should Judah *depend for protection* on a country that can't even defend itself?

b. All of Egypt's diversified economy—farming, fishing, and manufacturing—is dependent on the Nile. A serious drought could ruin every sector of the economy, bankrupting the nation. Why should Judah *depend for provision* on a country whose situation is this precarious?

c. Egypt was formerly renowned for the wisdom of its sages, but now they have become the same kind of staggering drunkards as the prophets and priests in Jerusalem. Why should Judah *depend for guidance* on a country whose counselors are so debauched? (They can get the same thing at home!)

➲ Judah's leaders saw Egypt as a revived empire with imposing military power, sustainable prosperity, and historic centers of learning. How do you think Isaiah was able to see through these appearances and predict (in the last part of this oracle) that Egypt would be conquered by Assyria? What appearances does a person need to see through today in order to give their allegiance to the individuals and communities who are truly furthering God's purposes?

2 The fourth part of Isaiah's prophecy against Egypt characteristically offers a promise of restoration in the midst of warnings of ruin. Isaiah envisions that, as unbelievable as it may seem, Egypt and Assyria will one day worship the Lord together with the people of Israel. By depicting the two great empires of his day, one at the western end and the other at the eastern end of his civilization, as people of faith, Isaiah reprises his vision of all nations streaming to Mount Zion to learn of God's ways. This prophecy had a partial fulfillment in the years after the exile, when Jewish colonies remained in Egypt and Babylon (the empire that succeeded Assyria), spreading the knowledge of the true God in both places. But its ultimate fulfillment will come in the more distant days that Isaiah also foresaw.

➲ In the 1950s Billy Graham and his close friends began praying that he would one day preach the good news about Jesus in Moscow, then the capital of the Soviet Union—as impossible as this seemed in those early and terrifying days of the Cold War. Dr. Graham lived to see this prayer answered. What nation or group of people is the hardest for you to envision coming to faith in Jesus? What would it look like if they did? Can you commit to praying regularly for them, remembering God's purposes for all nations as expressed in Isaiah's visions of the future?

3 The last part of this prophecy gives one more compelling reason why Judah should not make an alliance with Egypt: Under Assyrian pressure, the Egyptians have already abandoned and betrayed those who've depended on them. This reveals their true helplessness against the dominant empire.

In the previous session you saw how the Philistines revolted in 714 BC. With Egyptian backing, the Philistines in the city of Ashdod deposed their Assyrian-appointed ruler and proclaimed a man named Yamani their king instead. When the revolt was crushed, Yamani fled to Egypt for safety. But when the Assyrian armies demanded his surrender, the Egyptians simply tied him up and turned him over.

In light of these events, Isaiah predicts that the Egyptians and Cushites (Nubians) themselves will one day be conquered and led away captive to Assyria. (This prediction was fulfilled within fifty years.) This is why Isaiah envisions the smaller nations of the region saying, "See what has happened to those we relied on, those we fled to for help and deliverance from the king of Assyria! How then can we escape?" It's also why Isaiah is so opposed to his own nation depending on Egypt.

➲ The prophets often acted out the messages God was sending through them. In this case, to portray the future Egyptian and Cushite captives, Isaiah goes "stripped and barefoot" for three years. This action has raised serious concerns for many readers and students of the Bible. Would God really tell one of his own prophets to walk around naked for so long? Some scholars believe that Isaiah acted out this sign only on a one-time basis at the beginning of the revolt, three years before the fall of Ashdod. Others suggest that he was not completely naked, but rather in his undergarments. The vocabulary and syntax of the passage allow for both of these possibilities. However, it's equally likely that Isaiah did walk around naked for three years as a sensational warning against an Egyptian alliance. (In this culture nakedness was not always sexually provocative; here it represents the shame of conquest and captivity.) If God really did tell Isaiah to go around naked for three years, what do you make of this?

➲ If you needed to convey a warning from God today, what approach would command the greatest public attention?

4 Despite the prophet's warnings, and despite Egypt's betrayal of Yamani, members of the Judean royal court decided to pursue an alliance with the Egyptians. They did this secretly, probably to keep the Assyrians from finding out until their arrangements were finalized. They didn't consult Isaiah. But he knew what they were doing, and he brought their secret plans into the light.

Go back to Part Four and have someone read the third woe against Judah, which begins, "Woe to those who go to great depths to hide their plans from the LORD."

In this oracle Isaiah first expresses his amazement that anyone would think they could keep what they were doing a secret from God. He then announces that Judah's leaders, who have "turned things upside down" by acting as if they had more knowledge than the LORD, will soon find things turned upside down within their own kingdom. Those who have prospered through injustice and oppression will be swept away, while God will empower the weak and the needy. The kingdom will be preserved not by secret alliances with untrustworthy nations, but through a renewal of faith and justice. This prophecy began to be fulfilled in the religious and social reforms that Hezekiah introduced, and it has had further partial fulfillments in many other times and places. But its ultimate fulfillment still awaits the time when God will renew all things.

➲ Are you doing something that you're trying to keep a secret from everyone? Are you acting as if not even God knows what you're doing and won't let you get caught? If this is such a good idea, why don't you want anyone to know about it? If you realize that you need to give up a secret plan or activity, speak confidentially with someone who can help you do this and hold you accountable as you pursue a new way of life. Without asking people to identify themselves, pray together as a group for anyone in this situation.

SESSION 10

THE REVOLT AGAINST ASSYRIA IN 705–701 BC

Book of Isaiah > Part Four: Woes Against Judah > Fourth and Fifth Woes

INTRODUCTION

When the powerful Assyrian emperor Sargon was killed in battle in 705 BC, many of the nations the Assyrians had subjugated saw this as an opportunity to make a renewed bid for freedom. In the eastern part of the empire, Babylon and its allies rose up under the leadership of Marduk-Baladan. In the west, many of the nations that the Egyptians had been carefully cultivating similarly revolted. The biblical book of Samuel-Kings records that at this time King Hezekiah of Judah "rebelled against the king of Assyria and did not serve him."

But within two years, the new Assyrian emperor Sennacherib won a decisive victory against the Babylonians and their allies. Marduk-Baladan fled to the marshes of lower Mesopotamia for safety. Sennacherib then led a huge army against the rebel coalition in the west. The Judeans appealed urgently to Egypt for help. They were counting especially on horses and chariots they could use against the Assyrian invaders. During these desperate days Isaiah pronounced two more woes against the people of Judah. You'll read and discuss them in this session.

READING AND DISCUSSION

1 Have six people read the fourth woe against Judah, beginning at these places:

- "'Woe to the obstinate children,' declares the LORD"
- "A prophecy concerning the animals of the Negev"
- "Therefore this is what the Holy One of Israel says"
- "This is what the Sovereign LORD, the Holy One of Israel, says"
- "People of Zion, who live in Jerusalem, you will weep no more"
- "See, the Name of the LORD comes from afar"

In this oracle Isaiah describes Judean princes and envoys bringing gifts to Egypt to seek assistance. Because the Assyrians have already secured the Mediterranean coastline to block the flow of supplies and communications within the rebel coalition, the Judeans have to travel through the Negev desert to reach Egypt. This, in itself, should show them what a perilous foreign policy they're pursuing. But they've stopped consulting the LORD through his prophets; in fact, they've ordered Isaiah not to speak to them any more.

So God instructs Isaiah to make a large placard that reads "Rahab the Do-Nothing." (You'll recall from session 3 that Isaiah made a similar placard to announce the birth of his son Maher-Shalal-Hash-Baz.) Rahab was the chaos monster, symbolized by the forces of the sea. The Israelites sometimes applied the name to Egypt because God had defeated that country's armies at the Red Sea when he freed his people from being slaves there. Isaiah's placard exposes this supposedly fearsome empire as a worthless ally who will sit idly by when Judah is in danger. (It recalls the way Egypt betrayed and abandoned Yamani a few years earlier.) God also tells Isaiah to record his predictions on a scroll, so that in "the days to come," when these things happen, the people will realize that God has been trying to help them all along.

Isaiah says (or writes) that Judah's present policy will end in disaster: The nation will be shattered like a collapsed wall or a smashed piece of pottery. Nevertheless, he insists, "the LORD longs to be gracious to you." He promises that if the people will only cry out to God for help, he will rescue them. Isaiah describes how God will send them renewed guidance (even though they've defied his every word so far), prosperity, light, and joy. The oracle concludes with a prediction that God will come in awesome power to shatter

Assyria and with a description of how the rescued Judeans will sing for joy at this deliverance.

➲ Why do you think God kept promising to forgive and rescue the people of Judah, even when they became so defiant that they refused to listen to him anymore? (One possibility to consider: What was at stake for the rest of the world if Judah was obliterated?)

➲ What is one of the most remarkable experiences you've ever had of God's deliverance? What song would you choose to sing to celebrate this experience?

➲ Has someone you know decided that they don't want to hear anything more about God's wishes for their life? If so, take a few moments to compose a letter in your head that you would want to show them if they ever became open to God's influence again. Let this letter also be a prayer to God on their behalf. (If you wish, you can write an actual letter when you get home, but don't send it now—save it for "the days to come." Wait to see how God acts in the situation, and if this person does become more open to hearing your thoughts, share them then.) As Isaiah does in this oracle, stress how eagerly God wants to be gracious to them and bless them, but also include appropriate warnings about where their present course of life will lead. After this time of reflection, have one person lead the group in prayer for all of the unnamed people these mental letters have been composed for.

2 Have four people read the fifth woe against Judah, beginning at these places:

- "Woe to those who go down to Egypt for help"
- "This is what the Lord says to me"
- "See, a king will reign in righteousness"
- "You women who are so complacent, rise up and listen to me"

This fifth woe is similar in many ways to the fourth one, except that now the Assyrian threat is even closer. The last part of this oracle seems to reflect an occasion when Isaiah came across a group of women celebrating a harvest festival, apparently without a shred of concern over the danger the nation was in. He warned them that at this time next year there would be no harvest—the Assyrians would have laid waste to the land by then.

Like the preceding oracle, this one warns again of the folly of trusting in Egypt; it portrays God coming in power to defeat the Assyrians; and it foresees the blessed conditions the restored land will enjoy. But it develops two other shared themes at greater length.

First, it contrasts the scheming of Judah's royal counselors with the righteous and noble plans the Lord has for the nation. "He too is wise," Isaiah notes, in an ironic understatement. He uses wordplay to suggest that the people currently can't tell the difference between a fool (*nabal*) and a noble (*nadab*). But under a righteous king, their closed eyes will be opened and their stopped ears will hear once again, and they will be able to distinguish truth from error. The righteous king envisioned may initially be Hezekiah, who (as we'll see next time) eventually demoted the pro-Egyptian officials in his court and appealed directly to God for deliverance. But this prophecy also looks ahead to the Messiah.

A second theme this oracle emphasizes is the need for God's people to live not in complacency, or in misplaced trust in earthly agents, but in *quietness*—a calm, confident, well-placed trust in God. The previous oracle tells them similarly, "In repentance [returning to God] and rest is your salvation, in *quietness* and trust is your strength," just as Isaiah had told Ahaz over thirty years earlier, "*keep calm*" (the same word in Hebrew) "and don't be afraid."

➲ Why do you think the Judean royal court was dominated at this time by people Isaiah considered fools, rather than by more noble leaders? How can a person today tell whether the advice someone is giving them is foolish (that is, God-defying) rather than righteous (respectful of God)?

➲ What are the danger signs that a person is complacent, or is trusting in the wrong things, rather than enjoying the quietness of well-placed trust in God?

➲ What would more spiritual quietness look like in your life: Less anxiety? Greater freedom from worrying? Less need to scheme and manipulate? More readiness to turn to God? Greater patience in waiting on God? Something else? What can a person do practically to cultivate the kind of turning to God, resting, being quiet, and trusting that Isaiah describes?

FOR FURTHER READING AND DISCUSSION

The prophecies in Part Two against the Desert by the Sea, Dumah, and Arabia (which come right after the prophecy against Egypt that you considered in session 9) refer to the revolt in 705 BC of Babylon and its allies against Assyria. The Desert by the Sea is a title for Babylon itself. Dumah was an oasis on the caravan route between Babylon and Seir (Edom), Judah's southern neighbor. The settlements mentioned in Arabia, including Dedan, Tema, and Kedar, were also strategically located on trade routes. (See map, p. 24.) Babylon needed to depend on these southern allies to maintain communications and transportation links with its partners to the west, since the Assyrians controlled the northern routes. These prophecies express Isaiah's dismay as he foresees the defeat of Babylon and its allies in the east and the reprisals that will inevitably follow in the west against Egypt and its allies, including Judah.

The prophecy against Tyre is the last one in Part Two. Tyre was a wealthy and influential trading city on the Mediterranean coast. It and the nearby city of Sidon were ruled at this time by King Luli, who controlled much of the surrounding territory. He joined in the rebellion against the Assyrians. This prophecy describes how he fled to the island of Cyprus to escape their advancing armies after the Babylonians were defeated.

Read these prophecies against the Desert by the Sea, Dumah, Arabia, and Tyre and see what more they reveal about what various countries experienced as the Assyrians put down the revolt at both ends of their empire. Where does Isaiah see God at work in the events of these years?

ASSYRIA DEMANDS JERUSALEM'S SURRENDER

Book of Isaiah > Part Two: Prophecies Against the Nations > The Valley of Vision
Book of Isaiah > Part Six: Historical Narratives > The Assyrian Invasion

INTRODUCTION

According to Sennacherib's records, the Assyrian army reached the Mediterranean coast at the city of Sidon and worked its way southward toward Egypt, neutralizing all opposition along the way. The Egyptians marched north to meet them. The two armies battled at Eltekeh, a coastal city just north of Philistia. (See the map on p. 24.) The Egyptians were defeated and retreated to their own land. Judah was left to face the Assyrian onslaught alone.

READING AND DISCUSSION

1 Isaiah's prophecy against the Valley of Vision is actually spoken to Jerusalem. The prophet describes this city as if it were in a valley, even though it sits on a mountain, because the people's responses to their situation are so short-sighted it's as if their view is blocked on every side. "Vision" is an ironic name indicating that there's really no vision at all.

This prophecy depicts the situation in Jerusalem as its people are anticipating an imminent Assyrian siege of their city. It's found in Part Two of the book, just before the final prophecy against Tyre. (While the oracles in this part of the book are mostly against other nations, they can also address Judah, just as the woes against Judah sometimes speak to other nations.) Have two people read this prophecy, beginning at these places:

- "What troubles you now, that you have all gone up on the roofs?"
- "This is what the Lord, the LORD Almighty, says: 'Go, say to this steward, to Shebna the palace administrator . . .'"

King Hezekiah is doing what he can to fortify the city and secure its water supply for the upcoming siege. But the situation is desperate. Horses and chariots such as the people have been counting on are filling the land—but they belong to the enemy. The Assyrian divisions include warriors from Elam and Kir, evidence that these distant countries, who were allies with Babylon in the recent revolt, have been subjugated again.

Some of Jerusalem's defenders are fleeing the city, only to be captured immediately by the Assyrians. The rest of the people are throwing a city-wide end-of-the-world party, feasting and carousing. "Let us eat and drink," they exclaim, "for tomorrow we die!" The prophet can only weep bitterly over what seems like the inevitable destruction of his people because of their inadequate courage and preparations and their brazen hedonism in the face of judgment.

➲ This prophecy illustrates the various responses people make to a situation that feels overwhelming. Suppose that you're married and that you and your spouse are expecting a baby. Late in the pregnancy your doctors become concerned. After doing some tests they tell you that the baby is likely to be handicapped, perhaps severely. What would it look like in such a situation for you to

- run away?
- turn to substance abuse and escapism?
- get all the information and make all the preparations you can, but without depending on God?
- gather information and make preparations, but trust primarily in God for wisdom, strength, faith, and courage?

2 Shebna is the highest-ranking official in Judah under the king. It appears he has been one of the chief advocates for an Egyptian alliance, since Isaiah speaks of him taking pride in chariots. Shebna's response to the impending siege is to carve out a magnificent tomb for himself on a rocky height above the city. He expects in this way to make his name live on forever even after Jerusalem is destroyed (assuming, of course, that someone will actually bury him there). On God's instructions Isaiah goes to see him personally at the work site and declares that he will lose his position. It will be given to a man named Eliakim instead, who will be a mainstay of the community throughout the crisis, even though his responsibilities will prove to be more than one person can handle alone. Shebna himself will die in exile, his policy discredited and his grandiose fatalism a final disgrace to his honor.

➲ Do you know of any people who have created physical monuments to themselves, as Shebna was attempting to do here? If so, describe these for the group.

➲ Do you know anyone who doesn't have a great physical memorial, but whose legacy is the faith and courage they showed by honorably fulfilling a position of responsibility in a dangerous and deadly situation? If so, share their story with the group.

3 We'll now move to Part Six of the book of Isaiah and look at its first narrative, which relates the events that took place right after the ones described in the prophecy against the Valley of Vision. After the Assyrians defeated the Egyptian army at Eltekeh, they besieged the nearby Judean city of Lachish. They wanted to neutralize this fortress so it couldn't support a possible Egyptian counterattack. During the siege of Lachish, the Assyrian emperor Sennacherib sent his field commander to demand Jerusalem's surrender.

In session 1 you read the opening part of this first narrative to help you understand the background to the book. Now you'll see how this episode turned out. Have six people read the whole account out loud like a play, including the part you read in session 1. (It begins, "In the fourteenth year of King Hezekiah's reign . . .") Read all of Isaiah's prophecy and end with the short epilogue that explains what happened to Sennacherib in the end. Have the readers take these parts:

- Narrator
- The Assyrian field commander
- Eliakim, Shebna, and Joah (One person can speak their shared lines. Notice that, just as Isaiah predicted, Eliakim is now the palace administrator instead of Shebna, the man who was building himself a great tomb.)
- Isaiah
- Sennacherib's messengers (One spokesperson can read his message.)
- King Hezekiah

Ancient sources confirm the main details of this account. In his own records, Sennacherib boasts that he shut up Hezekiah "like a caged bird in Jerusalem, his royal city." Significantly, he doesn't boast, as he does of other opponents, that he destroyed him. Other ancient sources suggest that much of the Assyrian army was wiped out by a plague on this campaign. This may be what the biblical account means when it says that the angel of the LORD went out and killed so many soldiers. Assyrian records confirm that Sennacherib was murdered by two of his sons and succeeded by Esarhaddon. This murder actually occurred twenty years after the events described in this account; it's recorded here to show that Isaiah's prophecy came true.

While, on the surface, this appears to be a military contest, in essence it's really a spiritual one. Sennacherib and his commander insist that the kings of Assyria are more powerful than all the gods of the nations—including the God of Israel. Hezekiah prays for deliverance not primarily so that he and his people can be spared, but "so that all the kingdoms of the earth may know that you, LORD, are the only God." God tells him in response, through Isaiah, "I will defend this city and save it, for my sake and for the sake of David my servant!"—that is, for the sake of God's own reputation and that of his covenant promises, which will ultimately offer salvation to the whole world.

➲ As God's opponents in this situation, the Assyrians use diabolical means to try to get the Judeans to surrender without a fight. Where in this account do you see them using each of the following tactics against the people of Jerusalem?

- Humiliating them by reminding them of their failed strategies

- Ridiculing them by describing their weakness and lack of ability
- Claiming to be on God's side against them
- Acting as if they know all about them
- Terrorizing them with depictions of how bad it will be if they resist
- Trying to turn them against their leader
- Buying them off with promises of what they'll get if they surrender
- Trying to create a distrust of God

➲ Do you recognize times when God's spiritual opponents have used tactics like these against you, to try to get you to surrender without a fight? If so, share your experience with the group if you can.

➲ God defeats his opponents by using some distinctive tactics of his own. Where in this account do you see God working through the following means?

- Speaking through prophecy
- Responding to prayer
- Getting opponents to believe rumors that seem to confirm their worst fears
- Acting in overwhelming power

Take a moment to think about any experiences you've had in which you've seen God work through means like these and share them with the group if you can.

FOR FURTHER READING AND DISCUSSION

The second and sixth woes in Part Four of the book predict the invasion by the Assyrians and the sudden destruction of their army. In session 1 you noted where each of these woes begins.

The second woe calls the city of Jerusalem by the name Ariel, which means "altar hearth," that is, the place where sacrifices are offered. This may be a reference to the way the city was the center of the nation's worship. God protests through Isaiah, "These people . . . honor me with their lips, but their hearts are far from me." In other words, they've been serving God only superficially. However, the Assyrian invasion will make them think much more seriously about God, and they'll be astonished by his reality and power when he comes dramatically to deliver them.

The sixth woe begins by announcing directly to Assyria that it will be destroyed. Isaiah prays for strength and then proclaims that, even though the situation is now dire, God will come and deliver his people. The nation will have a rebirth of justice and God's power will be acknowledged by those far and near.

Read these two oracles and appreciate their details and overall message in light of what you've learned in the past few sessions about the Assyrian invasion and its unexpected ending.

SESSION 12

GOD'S JUDGMENT AGAINST ASSYRIA AND THE SURVIVAL OF A REMNANT IN JUDAH

Book of Isaiah > Part One > Closing Oracles

INTRODUCTION

Over the past several sessions we've explored the events that led up to the Assyrian invasion of Judah and the destruction of Sennacherib's army. We can now return to Part One of the book of Isaiah and consider the remaining oracles there, which all relate to the end of the Assyrian crisis.

These oracles begin right after the complex one you considered in session 6. They're grouped together on the basis of their common subject, and they're ordered by the book's characteristic catch phrase principle. For example, the term "remnant" ("remaining" in the NIV) is used at the end of the first oracle and at the beginning of the second one; the second oracle ends with an image of trees being cut down while the third one begins with the image of a stump; and so forth.

READING

Have different people take turns reading the concluding oracles of Part One of the book of Isaiah, beginning at the following places:

- "Woe to the Assyrian, the rod of my anger, in whose hand is the club of my wrath!"

- "In that day the remnant of Israel, the survivors of Jacob."
- "A shoot will come up from the stump of Jesse; from his roots a Branch will bear fruit."
- "In that day the Root of Jesse will stand as a banner for the peoples."
- "In that day you will say: 'I will praise you, LORD'" (ending, "great is the Holy One of Israel among you").

DISCUSSION

1 These poetic oracles confirm many of the details found in the narrative accounts of the Assyrian invasion. For example, they show the Assyrians citing their conquests of places such as Hamath, Arpad, and Samaria as evidence that their kings are greater than the gods of the nations and expressing their expectation that the God of Jerusalem will be no match for them, either. These oracles also describe how God will "send a wasting disease" upon the "sturdy warriors" of Assyria—a further suggestion that the angel of the LORD described in the historical account was the instrument of a plague.

God wanted to use Assyria to chasten his people, and he was even willing for these invaders to take plunder ("quick to the plunder, swift to the spoil"). But God didn't want them to completely obliterate other nations. However, the Assyrians did this, using their power and advantages excessively, because of their pride. "By the strength of my hand I have done this," they boasted. And so, Isaiah announces, God's judgment will now fall on them.

➲ What would it look like today for people in the following positions to make excessive use of their power?

- A head of state
- A military commander
- An employer
- An athletic coach
- A parent
- A pastor, elder, or other spiritual leader
- Someone else you can think of

How do people use power differently when they recognize it as something that God has entrusted to them—as the Assyrians failed to do?

➲ How can people keep from taking personal credit for what God has done through them, and so be spared the destructive effects of pride?

2 The oracle in the center of this group describes how Israel, regathered and reunited under a king from the lineage of Jesse (David's father), will bring blessing to the whole world. (The largest dispersion of Judeans was still in the future, but already many people from both the northern and southern kingdoms had been deported from their land.)

This is one of the most famous passages in the book of Isaiah. It vividly depicts predators like wolves and lions living peacefully with the animals that are usually their prey. It also describes children playing harmlessly with poisonous snakes. Some interpreters understand this portrait symbolically, as a figurative illustration of peace among the nations of the earth. But others take it more literally, expecting that the effects of the Messianic reign will extend even to a transformation of the natural world.

This oracle may have had a faint early fulfillment in the religious and legal reforms that King Hezekiah introduced. But given the dramatic and worldwide effects it anticipates, its true fulfillment must be expected in the time when the Messiah who came first as a suffering servant returns as a righteous king. (You'll hear much more about these two roles as we consider the later parts of the book.)

➲ The LORD's fundamental complaint against Israel here in Part One has been that the nation is guilty of injustice. The king described in this oracle has the qualities needed to uphold justice throughout his realm and beyond. What specific injustices in our world would you want to correct first, if you had the wisdom and the power to do so?

➲ How will the earth be different when it is filled with the knowledge of the Lord?

➲ Say whether you agree or disagree with the following statement, and why: "Followers of Jesus should express their faith in his coming Messianic reign by working now to bring about, even if only in specific places and times, the kinds of conditions that will prevail worldwide then."

3 Part One concludes with two short songs that praise the LORD for his mercy and salvation. They express the same wish that Hezekiah made during the darkest moments of the Assyrian invasion: that the LORD's name would be made known among all the nations. This happens both through remarkable acts of power such as the deliverance of Jerusalem and through songs like these that commemorate those acts. The people of Judah still have many difficult experiences ahead of them, as we'll discover in the following sessions. But at this moment in their history Isaiah can pause to compose these songs of praise to help his generation and future generations, including our own, remember and celebrate the character of God as revealed in the remarkable events of his time.

➲ What song or songs capture for you some of the most memorable experiences you've had of God's greatness and mercy? As a group, sing together some of the songs that people mention, or listen to recordings of them or watch video performances online.

FOR FURTHER READING AND DISCUSSION

In Part Two of the book of Isaiah, the second prophecy is a brief one against Assyria. (You noted it in session 1; it begins, "The LORD Almighty has sworn, 'Surely, as I have planned, so it will be.'") This prophecy echoes the language of the second oracle you read for this session. It says, for example, that Assyria's yoke will be lifted off the shoulders of God's people. Interpreters differ in their understandings of when and why this prophecy was composed. It may possibly be a shortened version of the oracle in Part One, designed to circulate more widely.

➲ How does this prophecy respond to the Assyrians' claim that their kings were greater than the gods of the nations?

Part Three of the book describes judgments that are worldwide in scope, affecting even the created order. It's difficult to determine what specific historical situation inspired the oracles in this part of the book. However, the third and fourth oracles have some themes in common with the two short praise songs at the end of Part One. They express the hope that God's anger will shortly pass and that all nations will learn about God from what he does for his people. The fourth oracle also echoes the song of the vineyard earlier in Part One.

➲ In session 1 you noted where Part Three began. Turn there now and read the third and fourth oracles, which begin "In that day this song will be sung in the land of Judah" and "In that day, the Lord will punish with his sword" (ending, "Those who were perishing . . . will come and worship the Lord on the holy mountain in Jerusalem"). How do these oracles express hope and trust even in a time of defeat and uncertainty about the future?

SESSION 13

THE SHADOW OF BABYLON LOOMS ON THE HORIZON

Book of Isaiah > Part Six > Hezekiah's Illness and the Envoys from Babylon

INTRODUCTION

As noted in session 1, just over half of the book of Isaiah (Parts One through Six) relates to the Assyrian crisis that culminated with the destruction of Sennacherib's army. The other half of the book (Parts Seven and Eight) deals with another crucial period in the history of Israel over 150 years later. In this session we'll see how the book of Isaiah makes the transition between these two periods.

Babylon, which had been crushed by the Assyrians in the revolt of 705 BC, eventually reestablished itself. It ultimately defeated Assyria and became the dominant empire in the region. It attacked and conquered its former ally Judah, destroying Jerusalem in 587 BC and carrying off much of the population into exile. But in the decades that followed, the Babylonians were threatened by other rising powers. The Medes and Persians to the east, led by the great general Cyrus, achieved a series of brilliant conquests that by 540 BC made them a threat to the city of Babylon itself. Would this city and its empire fall? And if it did, would Cyrus allow the Judeans to return home, as he had done for other captive populations that had come under his control? It would take great faith for the exiles to believe that God would allow them to go back and rebuild their society and nation, and even greater faith for them actually to do this. The second half of the book of Isaiah begins by placing this challenge before them.

The book uses another account from King Hezekiah's life to make the transition between its two halves. This account is rooted in the events of the Assyrian crisis but it also looks ahead to the Babylonian captivity. We'll consider it in this session, along with the prophecy against Babylon in Part Two of the book, which predicts the downfall of that empire and the return of the exiles.

READING AND DISCUSSION

1 Have three people read the account of King Hezekiah's illness and the visit from the Babylonian envoys. It's in Part Six, and it comes right after the story of the destruction of Sennacherib's army that you read in session 11. Have the readers start at these places:

- "In those days Hezekiah became ill and was at the point of death."
- "A writing of Hezekiah king of Judah after his illness and recovery."
- "At that time Marduk-Baladan son of Baladan king of Babylon sent Hezekiah letters and a gift" (ending with, "There will be peace and security in my lifetime").

This account is out of sequence historically. The events it describes most likely occurred a couple of years before the Assyrians invaded Judah. Their armies are already a threat, but Hezekiah's storehouses are still full. (The biblical book of Samuel-Kings records that once Sennacherib did invade, Hezekiah sent him a huge tribute to try to keep him from attacking Jerusalem.) The Judean king receives the Babylonian envoys "gladly" (literally he "rejoices" to see them), perhaps because he is relieved to learn that Marduk-Baladan is still alive and trying to keep the rebel coalition together even after his defeat by the Assyrians. All of this suggests a date around 703 BC. But the account of Hezekiah's illness is placed after the account of the Assyrian invasion because the visit from the Babylonian messengers foreshadows the Babylonian captivity, which will be the setting for the oracles in Part Seven.

Hezekiah is about forty years old at this time, but he still has no heir. This is why he says in his song that his "house" is being pulled down and taken away. (His son and successor Manasseh would only be born a few years later.) His deadly illness, in the face of the Assyrian threat, makes it appear that the dynasty of David and the nation of Israel are both doomed to extinction. This is probably why Hezekiah weeps so bitterly and finds death so hard to accept—he would be dying without hope. In response to his prayers and tears, God declares that he will spare his life and deliver the city and nation.

God offers a remarkable sign to confirm this promise. God makes the shadow cast by the sun change course and go ten steps back up a staircase to the palace. It's not clear by what means this was achieved. Biblical accounts suggest it was not a worldwide phenomenon (and so did not involve a means such as temporarily reversing the earth's rotation): The book of Chronicles records that the Babylonian envoys also came to inquire about "the miraculous sign that had occurred in the land," meaning that they'd heard about it, but they hadn't experienced it in their own country. Whatever the explanation, this sign, Hezekiah's recovery, and Marduk-Baladan's continuing designs against the Assyrians all brought his emissaries to Jerusalem, where they saw the wealth that would one day be theirs.

➲ What's going on here: Why do you think God first says one thing to Hezekiah, and then tells him something different? Choose the answer that best expresses your thoughts, or give another answer of your own.

- **a.** God had decreed judgment against Jerusalem and wanted to spare Hezekiah the pain of seeing his kingdom destroyed. But when Hezekiah prayed for a reprieve, God was moved to change his mind and spare both him and the nation of Judah.
- **b.** God planned all along to heal Hezekiah and deliver Jerusalem. The announcement that Hezekiah would die was a tactic designed to draw out the good things that were in his heart for everyone to see.
- **c.** God needed to know before he spared Jerusalem that its king would turn to him in a crisis, so he put Hezekiah through this test beforehand.

➲ God says that he has heard Hezekiah's prayer and seen his tears. Do you think God gauges the sincerity of our prayers by the depth of our emotions? Is expressing emotion to God a form of prayer?

➲ If you knew you only had another fifteen years to live, what would you most want to do with those years? The fate of Jerusalem seems to be tied here to the life of Hezekiah. Who or what depends on the way you'll live your life in the years ahead?

➲ There's much debate among interpreters over Hezekiah's conclusion, "The word of the Lord you have spoken is good. . . . There will be peace and security in my lifetime." Is he saying that the destruction of his kingdom is all right with him, so long as he lives out his own days comfortably? Or is he acknowledging that the most a person can do is fulfill the purposes of God in their own generation, and expressing satisfaction that in this moment he has been able to intercede for the nation as its king? Ask for a volunteer from the group to advocate for each of these positions, choose another person as moderator, and hold a debate on the topic, "Hezekiah: Selfish or Savior?" The rest of the group can vote to determine the winner.

➲ Hezekiah's song follows the standard pattern for a biblical psalm of thanksgiving.[1] It begins with a description of the troubles he faced, it recalls his cry to God for help, it recounts how God acted to deliver him, and it ends with praise and worship. Using this same pattern, write your own song of thanksgiving to celebrate a memorable time when God delivered you. Share it with the group at a future meeting if you'd like.

1. To find out more about the various types of psalms in the Bible, see the study guide in this series *Psalms / Lamentations / Song of Songs.*

FOR FURTHER READING AND DISCUSSION

The prophecy against Babylon, the first one in Part Two of the book, foretells the destruction of that great city and its empire by the Medes and their allies. This event took place some 150 to 200 years after the events described in the other prophecies in this part of the book. The placement of the prophecy against Babylon at the head of the collection helps tie together the two halves of the book and define its character as a work that deals with two different but equally critical periods in the life of the nation. Read this prophecy to get a feel for the developments that freed the Judean exiles to return to their homeland.

➲ What other prophetic oracles in the book that you've read so far does this one recall for you?

➲ The prophet encourages his audience to join him in taunting Babylon over its downfall. Is it appropriate for this kind of sentiment to be expressed in the Bible?

➲ Many interpreters understand the words addressed near the end of this oracle to the "morning star" or "son of the dawn" to have a double reference, both to Babylon and to Satan, who wanted to be higher than God. What do you think of this interpretation?

As we noted in the previous session, it's difficult to determine what specific historical situation inspired the oracles in Part Three of Isaiah. However, its first two oracles announce and celebrate the destruction of a great city that many interpreters believe is Babylon, although these oracles also look forward to the time when God will judge the entire world. Turn again to Part Three and read the first two oracles, which begin "See, the Lord is going to lay waste the earth" and "Lord, you are my God; I will exalt you and praise your name" (ending, "he will bring them down to the ground, to the very dust").

➲ What qualities do these oracles praise God for, as demonstrated in his judgment of this unnamed oppressive city?

THE END OF THE BABYLONIAN EXILE

SESSION 14

THE RHAPSODY OF ZION REDEEMED

Book of Isaiah > Part Seven > First Section (Overview)

INTRODUCTION

Part Seven of the book of Isaiah addresses the community of Judean exiles in Babylon.[1] It encourages them to believe that, as incredible as this might seem, the Persians under Cyrus will not only defeat the Babylonians and take over their empire, but they will also allow deported peoples to return to their homelands.

As we'll see in this and the following sessions, the oracles in this part of the book appear to have been spoken by a living member of the Judean exile community in Babylon to his contemporaries. Indeed, the speaker describes how he interacted personally with his listeners and experienced rejection and persecution when many members of the community refused to believe his message. These oracles depend for much of their force on the speaker's ability to refer to words God spoke "long ago" through Isaiah that are now coming true. For these reasons, many interpreters believe that they are actually the words of a later prophet that have been added to the collection of oracles by Isaiah the son of Amoz. This study guide will take just that position: that the oracles in Part Seven were delivered by a living member of the Judean exile community in Babylon. We'll call him simply "the prophet." (Since he uses

1. In connection with this and the following sessions, you may wish to read the biblical book of Daniel, which gives a picture of what life was like for these exiles.

masculine grammatical forms when speaking of himself in Hebrew, we'll use masculine pronouns for him in English as well.)

For different reasons, other interpreters believe that Isaiah himself spoke all of the words in the book that bears his name. Both of these positions are held and defended by scholars who are equally committed to the inspiration and authority of the Bible as the word of God.[2] If you'd like to learn more about the reasons why scholars hold these two different views, see the appendix to this study guide.

Part Seven of the book of Isaiah has two major sections. In the second section the prophet works through the experience of being rejected by the community for his message. As he does, he achieves profound insights into God's redemptive plans for the world and the means God will use to accomplish them. We'll consider this second section in sessions 20–23.

But before that, we must experience the first section, in which the prophet, in a sustained series of oracles, presents an expansive vision of the magnificent possibilities that lie before the Judean exiles, if they will only return to the LORD and trust in his promises. Richard Moulton has described Parts Seven and Eight of Isaiah as the "Rhapsody of Zion Redeemed."[3] We'll use that title here for the first section of Part Seven, for which it seems particularly appropriate. Moulton used the term "rhapsody" in the technical sense of an effusive, lyrical composition built of individual components that have been worked together into a grand whole. (Think Gershwin's *Rhapsody in Blue*.) This part of the book of Isaiah is, like other parts, built out of individual oracles connected by similarities in language and imagery. However, it has been arranged in such a way that it can be experienced all at once as a free-flowing, unified composition. That's what we'll do in this session, before looking in more detail at its individual passages in the sessions that follow.

2. Accordingly, Raymond Dillard and Tremper Longman write in their *Introduction to the Old Testament* (Grand Rapids: Zondervan, 1994) that the question of the authorship of Isaiah "should not be made a . . . test for orthodoxy" (p. 275).

3. Richard Moulton, *The Modern Reader's Bible* (New York: Macmillan, 1907), p. 1393.

READING

Take turns reading through the Rhapsody of Zion Redeemed. It begins right after the story of the Babylonian envoys that you considered in session 13, with the words, "Comfort, comfort my people, says your God." It should take you about ten to fifteen minutes to read through to the ending: "'There is no peace,' says the LORD, 'for the wicked.'" (This comes shortly after the prophet calls out, "Leave Babylon, flee from the Babylonians!")

If you're using *The Books of the Bible*, change readers every time you come to one of the breaks that's marked by extra white space. If you're using another edition, change readers whenever you come to what feels like a natural literary break. When particular phrases or images strike you, try to remember them so you can share them later with the group.

As you read and listen, notice how, in this extended series of oracles, different motifs emerge, develop, submerge, and then surface again—much like the motifs in a symphony. They are skillfully interwoven to give the entire composition a complex unity. They include the following themes:

- None of the idols of the nations can compare with the LORD, the God of Israel. He is the Creator; he is the one who announces beforehand what will happen; he alone has the power to bring things to pass.
- By comparison, the nations and their idols are fleeting and insignificant, like withered grass or wind-blown chaff.
- God has completely forgiven the sins that caused the Judean exile.
- He will gather up the exiles and make a way through the desert for them to return home. He will rebuild Jerusalem in splendor and it will become a beacon for all nations.
- God has appointed a special servant to accomplish his redemptive purposes in the world. In one sense, this servant is the nation of Israel; in another sense, it's Cyrus; in yet another, it's the prophet who is speaking; and in an even further sense, it's an unnamed, future, humble, Spirit-filled figure.
- Unfortunately, the people of Israel, discouraged by their experience in exile, are spiritually deaf and blind. They don't recognize or believe that God is at work to redeem them. And

so God is speaking through his prophet to reawaken their spiritual senses.

As you listen, you'll also recognize many ways in which these oracles echo the language and themes of the first half of the book. For example, God often says here, as he did there, "Do not fear, for I am with you." Legal language is used once again as God says things like "Present your case," as the idols of the nations are put on trial and shown to have no claim to the people's allegiance. The vision from Part One of all nations streaming to Jerusalem is evoked in several places.

The overall message of this rhapsody is that the Lord wants his people first to return to him, and then to return to their land where they can be his servant to help accomplish his redemptive purposes for the whole world.

DISCUSSION

➲ What were your favorite lines within this extended series of oracles? Read them again for the group and explain why they were meaningful to you.

➲ What do you think of the title "The Rhapsody of Zion Redeemed"? What other title might you give to this part of the book?

➲ Picture yourself as a young Judean exile in Babylon. This is the only home you've ever known. The land your people come from is several hundred miles away and you probably wouldn't be able to reach it even if you were allowed to travel there. Some of your people have clung to their traditional faith, but many others have abandoned it. You've heard vaguely of an ancient prediction that one day you'll be free to return to your land. Now a prophet appears and announces that this prediction is about to come true, and when it does, the God who made the whole world will want you to uproot your life here and make the long and dangerous journey back to your homeland. You've just listened to everything he has to say. How do you respond? What hopes do his words awaken? What questions and concerns and struggles do you still have?

➲ What challenges do these words present to followers of Jesus today? What attitudes, beliefs, and activities do they critique? What opportunities and responsibilities do they identify? Do followers of Jesus have some contemporary role as the Lord's "servant," as that figure is depicted here?

➲ Conclude your time together, if you wish, by listening to some selections from Handel's *Messiah* that are based on Part Seven of Isaiah, such as the recitative "Comfort Ye My People," the air "Every Valley Shall Be Exalted," the chorus "And the Glory of the Lord Shall Be Revealed," and the air and chorus "O Thou That Tellest Good Tidings to Zion." (You can listen to recordings of these selections or watch videos of performances of them on the Internet.) Alternatively, to appreciate one way of thinking about the form of this extended passage, you can listen to George Gershwin's *Rhapsody in Blue*.

GOD CALLS A NEW PROPHET TO SPEAK TO THE EXILES

Book of Isaiah > Part Seven > First Section

INTRODUCTION

Now that you've experienced this section of the book as a whole, it's time to return to its individual oracles and consider them in more detail. The first few oracles set the stage for all that follows and introduce the main theme of the prophet's message.

READING AND DISCUSSION

1 Have someone read the first oracle in Part Seven, beginning "Comfort, comfort my people, says your God" and ending "he gently leads those that have young."

This opening passage may be an account of the prophet's call to bring God's word of forgiveness and restoration to his contemporaries. Interpreters have noted some interesting parallels between this passage and Isaiah's call to prophesy, which you considered in session 2.

- In both cases there's a search for someone to represent God. In Isaiah's vision in the temple, God asks, "Whom shall I send? And who will go for us?" In this passage God gives the command to comfort his people in the plural imperative, suggesting that it's addressed to all who hear in the hopes that someone will respond.

- In both cases the God who is looking for a representative is defined as the one whose glory is universal. The seraphs cry, "The whole earth is full of his glory." Here a voice calls, "The glory of the LORD will be revealed, and all people will see it together."
- In each case the prophet wonders how he can speak for God and questions whether the people will respond. Isaiah says, "Woe to me! . . . I am a man of unclean lips, and I live among a people of unclean lips." The prophet says here, "All people are like grass, and all their faithfulness is like the flowers of the field. The grass withers and the flowers fall." (The term "faithfulness" describes keeping a covenant loyally; the prophet recognizes how fickle the people are.)
- Both prophets are encouraged and empowered by an intermediary. A seraph touches Isaiah's lips with a coal from the altar. Here the voice that first echoes God's call for a representative encourages the later prophet to "cry out."
- In each case the message concerns the "cities" or "towns" of Judah. (The same Hebrew term is used in both passages.) But while Isaiah was told he would prophesy "until the cities lie ruined," the prophet here is told to "speak tenderly to Jerusalem," and so he tells the towns of Judah that their God is coming to rescue them.
- Both prophets must accept the difficult assignment of speaking to people who are not receptive to their message. In session 2 you discussed what it was like for Isaiah to accept such an assignment. The prophet here realizes that while humans can't be depended on, "the word of our God endures forever," and so it can still be proclaimed with hope and confidence.

➲ The most significant difference between the two accounts is that Isaiah is called when he sees a vision, while this prophet is called when he hears a voice. Ask the members of your group to go to one side of the room if they learn primarily by seeing, and to the other side of the room if they learn primarily by hearing. Then ask each person to describe what they do for a living or what some of their primary skills and activities are.

➲ What message does God have for the people of your place and time? What part can you play in helping to deliver this message? How do you think people are likely to respond? What encouragement can you find in these accounts of the prophets' callings to help you not to be afraid, even if you're concerned that this message will be unpopular?

2 Have someone read the next oracle in Part Seven, beginning "Who has measured the waters in the hollow of his hand . . . ?" and ending, "Because of his great power and mighty strength, not one of them is missing."

This oracle presents the prophet's essential message to the Judean exiles: The LORD, their God, is not only greater than the nations and their idols, but these cannot even be compared to him. And so the LORD is entitled to the exiles' renewed loyalty and complete trust as he works out his purposes for them.

This oracle begins by describing God's great power and wisdom. It then contrasts these with the insignificance of the nations, which include even the empires that are now competing for domination. The idols of the nations are exposed as mere human fabrications, in the first of several such mocking depictions in this section. God is the one who created everything, including people; the gods of the nations have been created by people. Finally, the oracle returns to celebrate God's power and supremacy once again.

➲ Who or what is a rival to God for the people of your culture as a source of meaning, security, or power? Assess this thing on the prophet's own terms: How did it come into being—who made it, and how? How long is it likely to be around? Is it worthy of being compared to God?

➲ The end of this oracle depicts the original creation being re-enacted every evening at dusk as God calls on the stars to appear. Stand outside one evening during the week ahead and watch the stars come out. Go to a place away from city lights so you can see this happening well. Imagine as each star becomes visible that it has just heard God call it by name and that it is shining in response. At your group's next meeting, share what this experience was like.

3 Have someone read the next oracle in Part Seven, beginning "Why do you complain, Jacob?" and ending, "they will run and not grow weary, they will walk and not be faint."

In this oracle we hear what the Judean exiles are saying about God. It can be summarized this way: "He's forgotten about us! He no longer cares what happens to us!" This may be the rebuff the prophet got when he first tried to tell the people God was going to rescue them, or it may be what they were already saying before he spoke to them. Either way, the prophet replies that God hasn't given up or grown tired of trying to help them. If they will hope in the Lord, waiting in confidence for him to act, their own strength will be renewed and they'll dare to go on the great adventure God is now calling them to.

➲ For what task do you most need a renewal of your strength right now so you can help accomplish God's purposes for the world? What difference would it make to believe, as the prophet tells the exiles here, that God hasn't given up on your enterprise? If you thought that God hadn't abandoned you, but was actively interested in equipping and empowering you, would this give you renewed energy and enthusiasm for this task?

➲ Conclude your time together, if you wish, by singing or listening to Don Moen's song "Like Eagles," which is based on this oracle.

SESSION 16

THE CASE AGAINST THE IDOLS OF THE NATIONS

Book of Isaiah > Part Seven > First Section, Continued

INTRODUCTION

In this session you'll continue considering the individual oracles that make up the Rhapsody of Zion Redeemed. You'll see the LORD take his rivals, the idols of the nations, to court and invalidate their credentials. You'll also be introduced to the "servant of the LORD," the unnamed figure whose future work the prophet anticipates and describes at several places in this part of the book.

READING AND DISCUSSION

1 Have someone read the next oracle in this section of the book. It begins, "Be silent before me, you islands!" and it ends, "Their deeds amount to nothing; their images are but wind and confusion."

This oracle describes a court proceeding between the LORD and the idols of the nations. The Judean exiles were tempted to depend on these idols because they believed that their own God had either abandoned them or could do nothing to help them. The LORD wants to reclaim the loyalty of those who should rightfully be trusting in him.

In ancient Israel a person who had a case against someone else could either let them speak first and then reply to them, or else initially present their own case and ask for a response. Here God tells the nations, meaning their gods, to listen while he speaks first, and then to marshal their best arguments in reply. On this basis, he urges them, "Let us meet together at the place of judgment."

The main evidence the LORD offers to demonstrate that he is the only true God, and thus the one whom Israel should worship, is that he planned and announced in advance the developments that are now shaking the world of the Babylonians. He appointed Cyrus, "one from the east" (Persia), to conquer their empire and liberate its captive peoples.

The LORD interrupts his argument to observe how the threatened nations, terrified, are banding together and making idols that they hope will deliver them. He addresses the people of Israel and tells them they don't need to be afraid; they will not be destroyed in the current conflict. Instead, he will protect them and bring them safely back to their home. (Here there is a reprise of the imagery from the first oracle in Part Seven of a highway through the desert.)

All of this, the LORD says in summary, is proof that he is the true God. He then invites the idols to respond: "Present your case. . . . Set forth your arguments." But the challenge is met only with silence. So the LORD makes some suggestions to the idols. How about mentioning some of the things you planned and announced long ago that are now taking place? Or describing some of the things you have in mind for the future? Silence still. "Do something—anything," God finally blurts out, "just so we'll know you're alive!" But the idols aren't alive. They don't just have a weak case; it's not that they have nothing to say; there's no one there to say anything. "You are less than nothing," God declares.

And so the LORD makes his closing argument. He reminds the court that he has stirred up Cyrus (who is now described as "from the north," since that's the direction from which he is threatening Babylon) and that he declared long before this that Babylon would fall and the Judean exiles would return home. "I gave to Jerusalem a messenger of good news," he explains—meaning Isaiah, who predicted this over 150 years earlier, beginning when he named his son Shear-Jashub, "a remnant shall return." None of the other so-called gods foretold any of this, and so they are not gods at all. The court must conclude that the Lord is "right"—not just right in what he has predicted, but in the right so far as this case is concerned. He alone is entitled to Israel's loyalty and devotion.

➲ If you were God's lawyer, how would you conduct his case in a trial like this today? What do you feel are the best evidences that could be presented for the unique reality of God, which no rival could answer?

➲ Once the Lord senses that his listening people are beginning to be persuaded that he is the only true God, he tells them not to be afraid and not to worry that he will forsake them. For you, what is frightening and risky about identifying God as the only being who should have, and must have, your unconditional allegiance?

2 Have someone read the next oracle, beginning with, "Here is my servant, whom I uphold" and ending with, "new things I declare; before they spring into being I announce them to you."

This oracle provides more evidence that the Lord is the only true God. He can meet both parts of the challenge he flung at the idols: Not only can he point to things he announced long ago that are happening now, he can also describe what will happen in the future.

In this oracle God speaks about what he will accomplish through a figure he identifies as his "servant." This term is applied frequently to the people of Israel in this part of the book; similar language is also used for Cyrus and for the prophet himself. But in passages like this one, which have become known as the "servant songs" in the book of Isaiah, the servant is an unnamed figure through whom God will work in the future to bring salvation to the whole world. This figure is the Messiah who has already been introduced in several of the oracles in Part One (sessions 3, 10, and 12).

Here we learn two things about the servant that are so unexpected no one would have anticipated them. But God knows these things in advance, and this demonstrates both God's reality and power and the servant's identity as God's agent. First, the servant will be gentle. Not weak—he will have a quiet but powerful strength. As the oracles in Part One also say, God's Spirit will be upon him. But unlike Cyrus, who smashes nations and kings into dust with his sword and bow, the servant will carefully bring restoration and healing. Second, even though the servant will come in connection with the LORD's covenant with Israel, he will be "a light for the Gentiles." He will establish justice on earth, for people of all nations. We'll learn much more about this servant in the sessions ahead.

➲ How is the servant's gentleness depicted in this oracle? Where is his strength, and the source of his strength, described? The New Testament explains that Jesus is the figure foretold in the servant songs of this book. If you're a follower of Jesus, how have you experienced his gentleness? His strength? His work of healing and restoration?

3 Have someone read the next oracle, beginning with "Sing to the LORD a new song" and ending with "those who trust in idols . . . will be turned back in utter shame."

The prophet responds to everything that has just been disclosed about the LORD and his purposes by calling on the whole earth to worship him together. He depicts how comprehensive this worship should be by showing it extending over a whole spectrum of geographic features. It begins down at the sea and then progresses to the "islands."

The term *islands* occurs frequently in this part of the book, including in all three oracles you've read for this session. It means literally "coastlands," lands along the coast, and so it includes territories on the shores of seas as well as islands offshore. It's often used in parallel with such terms as "the ends of the earth," and as a synonym for "the nations," as when God summons the idols into court. When the prophet uses this term, it indicates that his vision is extending to the farthest reaches of the inhabited world.

From the seacoast the song of praise moves inland to the settlements of the desert nomads (Kedar), then up to the rocky crags (Sela), and finally to the mountaintops. As it climbs in elevation it also swells in volume, until the whole world is "giv[ing] glory to the LORD." The prophet is envisioning the fulfillment of the proclamation that "the glory of the LORD will be revealed, and all people will see it together."

God answers this groundswell of praise by describing once more what he is about to do: He will act against the powerful oppressors of the world (represented, in similar geographic symbolism, by great mountains and rivers). He will open his people's eyes and light the way home for them. The oracle concludes with one more warning not to trust in idols.

➲ The prophet envisions the people of the whole world declaring their allegiance to the Lord through united worship. How would you respond to someone who said, "Sure, I believe in God, and I consider myself a follower of Jesus, but I don't see why I need to take part in worship gatherings"?

➲ As a group, can you describe how a wave of praise to God might sweep from the seacoast to the mountains, or even circle the earth, as people you know in various places join in worship gatherings? Decide where and when the wave you want to track will start and end, and identify people living all along the route who will be part of it at strategic points. Then have someone narrate its course from start to finish. Alternatively, if someone in the group is good at using social media, they can create a "Praise Wave" event and have people that your group members know in various parts of the world sign in sequentially from their worship gatherings one weekend.

SESSION 17

MERCY TRIUMPHS OVER JUDGMENT

Book of Isaiah > Part Seven > First Section, Continued

INTRODUCTION

The Rhapsody of Zion Redeemed next presents two pairs of oracles. In each case, the first oracle in the pair describes how Israel's own sins were the cause of its destruction and exile. This is in response to the people's charge that God has either given up on them or is unable to save them: The fault isn't God's, but their own. But then the second oracle in each pair answers the first one with promises of forgiveness and restoration. The LORD still loves his people and is working powerfully and actively to deliver them.

READING

Have two people read these pairs of oracles, with the first person reading the first oracle in each pair, and the second person responding by reading the second oracle, beginning at these places:

- (First Reader) "Hear, you deaf; look, you blind, and see!"
- (Second Reader) "But now, this is what the LORD says."
- (First Reader) "This is what the LORD says—your Redeemer, the Holy One of Israel."
- (Second Reader) "But now listen, Jacob, my servant, Israel, whom I have chosen" (ending with, "still others will write on their hand, 'The LORD's,' and will take the name Israel").

DISCUSSION

1 There's a beautiful symmetry between the oracles in each pair. In the first one the prophet describes the judgment the people have suffered. Then in the second one he promises restoration, echoing but repurposing the language he has just used:

First pair:

First oracle: The prophet says the people have become "plunder," "with no one to say, '*Send them back*,'" and that the nation was "enveloped . . . in *flames*" when foreign armies invaded it (emphasis mine throughout).

Second oracle: The Lord will now say to all of the nations where the people are held captive, "Give them up! *Do not hold them back*," and God promises, "When you walk through the fire, you will not be burned; the *flames* will not set you ablaze."

Second pair:

First oracle: Israel has become an object of scorn.

Second oracle: Everyone will be eager to identify with Israel.

➲ Do you know of someone who turned to God and then, over time, experienced a wonderful reversal of the consequences of their past mistakes, so that their life began to turn out much better? If so, tell their story to the group if you know they wouldn't mind.

2 The second oracle in each pair also picks up a *key image* from the first one and uses it in a new way.

First pair:

First oracle: The exiled people are God's *deaf* and *blind* servant. (The "servant" here is the nation, not the future deliverer or Messiah.) Many years before, Isaiah was sent to people who would listen but not hear and look but not see. Now deafness and blindness symbolize the way the exiles can't or won't understand that God has not abandoned them.

Second oracle: These people "who have eyes but are *blind*, who have ears but are *deaf*" are called to serve as witnesses for God in a court case. Even though they don't understand the meaning of their experiences, they can at least testify to what those experiences have been. This testimony establishes that God has "revealed and saved and proclaimed" in a way that no other so-called god has ever done.

Second pair:

First oracle: God will "provide *water* in the wilderness and *streams* in the wasteland, to give drink to my people." This demonstration of power is like the exodus, the time when God "made a way through the sea" to allow the Israelites to escape from slavery in Egypt.

Second oracle: God will "pour *water* on the thirsty land, and *streams* on the dry ground." In this case the symbol represents how God will pour out his Spirit on the exile community so that it will once again thrive and prosper.

It's possible that these four oracles were originally composed separately and that they were put in their present arrangement because of similarities in their language and imagery, as happens often throughout this book. But within this arrangement, through the interplay of words and symbols, the paired oracles vividly communicate a message of mercy triumphing over judgment. When a text takes on further meaning in the presence of another text, this phenomenon is known as intertextuality. We see this phenomenon in these pairs of oracles. We also see it in other oracles that have been brought together by catch phrases and thematic similarities, and between the two halves of the book. We also see it within the Bible as a whole, when New Testament writers recognize later fulfillments of prophecies in the events of their time.

➲ If someone is interested in finding out more about following Jesus, can a person be an effective witness to them simply by relating their own experiences as a follower of Jesus, even if they can't explain the meaning and purpose of some particular experiences they've had?

➲ If you believe that the Bible is the inspired Word of God, do you think that God inspires not just the original meanings of individual compositions, but also the further meanings they take on in the presence of other writings within the Scriptures? Do you feel that you've seen interpreters identify instances of intertextuality responsibly because they understood and respected the original contexts of individual passages? Have you seen interpreters draw connections between passages that didn't seem valid?

3 Each pair of oracles also features a trial scene—a device we've seen earlier in the book (in sessions 4, 5, and 14).

In the first pair of oracles:

The Lord challenges the gods of the nations to produce witnesses who can testify to times when they've announced something they were going to do in the future and then made this happen. The gods can produce no witnesses. But the Lord tells the people of Israel, "You are my witnesses." Their role as his servant and messenger includes testifying to all nations about his power and reality.

In the second pair of oracles:

God puts Israel itself on trial. The people don't understand why he has allowed them to be conquered and exiled when, as they see it, they've been faithful to him by maintaining the outward forms of religion, such as by offering sacrifices. God explains that it's not these outward forms he's really concerned about. (This is yet another echo of the themes of the first half of the book, where the Lord says, "I have no pleasure in the blood of bulls and lambs and goats.") Rather, God wants the people to live pure lives and practice justice in their communities. And so he takes them to court and challenges them to "state the case for your innocence," knowing that this proceeding will expose their sins of injustice and oppression and show them that these are responsible for the conquest and exile.

➲ Isaiah had a remarkable vision of God's law going forth from Zion so that all nations could learn his ways and "walk in his paths" (session 4). In response, Isaiah urged his own people, "Let us walk in the light of the Lord." In the oracles you read for this session, the prophet explains similarly that the Lord has made his law "great and glorious," but unfortunately his own people "would not follow his ways" (literally "walk in" them). As a result, instead of being witnesses of God's reality and power, they've become objects of scorn. In your opinion, when people are despised and ridiculed for following Jesus, instead of being honored and imitated, how much of this is due to an unjust world's natural antipathy toward the justice of God, and how much is due to the failure of Jesus' followers to live out their faith with integrity?

➲ The prophet says that when the Lord pours out his Spirit on his people, they will become so honored and respected that those of other nations will write on their hands, "The Lord's." Write this on your hand with a pen or marker and leave it on for at least a week. At your next meeting, share with the group what experiences you have as a result, and how it affects the way you deal with others around you.

FOR FURTHER READING AND DISCUSSION

Read the next oracle in the book, which begins, "This is what the LORD says—Israel's King and Redeemer, the LORD Almighty" and ends, "the LORD has redeemed Jacob, he displays his glory in Israel." Where does this oracle use the same language and imagery as the pairs of oracles you read for this session? How does it use these words and symbols in new ways? (For example, what different group of people does it describe as having eyes but being unable to see?) What scene does this oracle develop at length that's portrayed more briefly in other parts of the Rhapsody of Zion Redeemed?

SESSION 18

THE LORD'S UNEXPECTED DELIVERER

Book of Isaiah > Part Seven > First Section, Continued

INTRODUCTION

The prophet now reveals to his fellow Judean exiles the name of God's chosen deliverer. We've already identified him as the Persian emperor Cyrus. But to this point the prophet has only referred to him by descriptions, calling him, for example, someone whom God has "stirred up . . . from the east." To the extent that the people believe his promises, they're probably expecting this deliverer to be another great Israelite leader like Moses, who originally brought the nation out of captivity, or David, who defeated its enemies. Instead, the prophet now announces that God will use the pagan emperor Cyrus to free them and return them to their land. This announcement is God's formal commissioning of Cyrus as his chosen instrument to "rebuild my city [Jerusalem] and set my exiles free." God actually gives Cyrus the titles of "shepherd" and "anointed," which have always been reserved for Israel's own kings and priests.

This is too much for the exiles. They refuse to accept it. And so, in this extended oracle (possibly a combination of oracles), the Lord answers them back. He reminds them that they are finite mortals—"potsherds among the potsherds on the ground." God uses this kind of language to put the people back in their place, because they're presuming they know what God would do. Actually, they are in no position to second-guess the means and methods of the God who created the heavens and the earth. The Lord explains that his unexpected choice of a deliverer will have far-reaching effects. Once Jerusalem is rebuilt by the returned exiles, people from all nations will turn from their idols and acknowledge the true God. (The peoples are represented here by the Egyptians and their southern neighbors, the Cushites and Sabeans—inhabitants of the ends of the earth, from a Babylonian perspective.)

"Truly you are a God who has been *hiding* himself," these nations will say (emphasis mine). And in one sense this is true: The "God and Savior of Israel" chose to reveal himself first to a nation that was virtually insignificant on the world stage—not the place most people would look for the supreme God. But in another sense, God insists, "I have not spoken in *secret*" (the same Hebrew root as "hiding"). God revealed himself openly to Israel and called that nation to be his messenger to the other nations. If they will believe and trust him now, they can fulfill this calling, and people from the ends of the earth will turn to the LORD and be saved. "Before me every knee will bow," God says, "by me every tongue will swear."

READING

Have six people read this series of oracles for the group, beginning at these places:

- "This is what the LORD says—your Redeemer, who formed you in the womb."
- "This is what the LORD says to his anointed, to Cyrus."
- "Woe to those who quarrel with their Maker."
- "This is what the LORD says: 'The products of Egypt and the merchandise of Cush, and those tall Sabeans.'"
- "For this is what the LORD says—he who created the heavens, he is God."
- "Gather together and come; assemble, you fugitives from the nations," ending, "all the descendants of Israel will find deliverance in the LORD and will make their boast in him."

DISCUSSION

➲ The Lord says he will use Cyrus to deliver his people, and consequently to help all nations learn that he is the true God, even though Cyrus does not currently know or acknowledge him (although God does say he wants Cyrus to know him). Is it legitimate for God to use unbelievers as instruments of his redemptive purposes without their knowledge or consent?

➲ What about believers: Does God need to get their permission before working through them? Would finite mortals really be able to understand what God wanted to accomplish through them, so they could give informed consent?

➲ Do you think of the Lord as a "God who has been hiding himself," or rather as a God who has "not spoken in secret"? Where do you see God acting openly and transparently, disclosing his purposes, and where do you believe God is instead at work mysteriously behind the scenes?

➲ At the beginning of this series of oracles, the Lord introduces himself as the architect of creation, whose work in nature and history is so complex and intricate that would-be prophets and diviners, and often even "the wise," consistently guess wrong about his intentions and appear foolish. At the same time, God declares his plans through his servants and messengers (in this case meaning the prophets). While these plans may seem outrageous when first announced (anointing a pagan emperor?), over time the divine wisdom behind them becomes apparent. What predictions have you heard people make, supposedly on God's authority, that have ended up seeming foolish? On the other hand, have you ever discovered that there was divine wisdom behind a course of action that you felt led to take, even though you initially had serious reservations about it? Given all that we learn in the Scriptures about God's work over many centuries, why are God's future moves still so difficult to predict?

➲ What kind of plan for the future might God announce that you would find simply too much to believe?

"FLEE FROM THE BABYLONIANS!"

Book of Isaiah > Part Seven > First Section, Concluded

INTRODUCTION

The Rhapsody of Zion Redeemed concludes with a series of oracles in which the prophet continues to answer the people's objections to God's choice of Cyrus as their deliverer. These oracles culminate in a direct challenge, as the prophet tells the people they must make a definitive choice to trust and obey the God of Israel and abandon the idols of Babylon.

READING AND DISCUSSION

1 Have someone read the next oracle in the book, beginning with "Bel bows down, Nebo stoops low" and ending with "I will grant salvation to Zion, my splendor to Israel."

This oracle portrays the Babylonians trying to protect idols of their two main gods, Bel and Nebo, by carrying them away on the backs of draft animals as they flee from the invading Persians. This is a preliminary depiction of the downfall of Babylon, which will be pursued at greater length in the next oracle. But the main purpose of the image is to delegitimize the false gods and idols that many of the exiled Israelites have come to worship. Bel and Nebo will ultimately be "unable to rescue the burden," that is, to protect their own images along with those who worship them. While these false gods can't even be carried off successfully, the Lord has upheld and carried the people of Israel for their whole history, and will continue to do so into the future. The prophet says that the people should remember this and abandon their stubborn-hearted resistance. There can be no real rivalry, or even comparison, between a fabricated god and the true God, the Lord of history who is now using Cyrus to fulfill his purposes.

➲ Are you carrying something that should be carrying you? That is, are you continually having to prop up or bail out or make excuses for a relationship, a life arrangement, a belief system, etc., that supposedly provides confidence and security for you, but isn't really doing this? If so, how can you come to trust and depend instead on the God who has actually "upheld [you] since your birth" and "carried [you] since you were born"?

➲ What habits or practices can you cultivate to help you remember how God has worked in your life in the past and to anticipate how God will fulfill his purposes for you in the future, so that you can trust and depend on him when you find yourself in difficult circumstances?

2 Have someone read the next oracle, beginning with "Go down, sit in the dust, Virgin Daughter Babylon" and ending with "there is not one that can save you."

This oracle is a longer depiction of the downfall of Babylon. It begins with an extended portrayal of the imperial capital as a proud, complacent, delicate lady who is suddenly made homeless and has to live on the ground, and who is thrust into the unaccustomed role of doing hard manual labor to survive. The oracle then transitions into a series of mocking challenges to the Babylonians' pretensions to know and control the future through astrology and magic spells. While Babylon has had the audacity to say, as if it were God, "I am, and there is none besides me," it will soon discover that its wealth, power, and knowledge can't rescue it from the coming disaster.

➲ This oracle is a "taunt song" that describes God's judgment against an oppressive power and its ruling elites. In your own lifetime, when have you seen proud, oppressive rulers brought low? How have their former victims celebrated their demise?

➲ The prophet chastises the Babylonians for their pride, complacency, and love of luxury, as well as for their presumption that they can forecast the future and ward off disaster. To what extent do these same criticisms apply to your own society? (For example, in what kinds of "forecasting" does it place its confidence?) If you're part of a community of Jesus' followers, how well would you say it's doing at modeling the contrasting values of humility, concern, simplicity, and dependence on God?

3 Have someone read the next oracle, beginning with "Listen to this, you descendants of Jacob" and ending with "I will not yield my glory to another."

In this oracle the prophet addresses the exile community once again. They "claim to rely on the God of Israel," but they're not really doing so "in truth or righteousness." Their actions are not right, and their relationship with God is not right, because they're still torn between loyalty to God and allegiance to idols. So the prophet renews an argument he's been making all along: God announced long in advance that he would bring the people back from exile, so that when this happened, the people couldn't credit some other god for their deliverance. But the prophet now makes a new argument as well. He says that he is also going to tell the people new things, which they "have not heard of . . . before today," so that when these things happen, they won't be able to say, "I knew of them," and dismiss them as nothing remarkable or unexpected. In other words, God announced some of his plans in advance (through Isaiah), in order to be given credit for them when he accomplished them. But he didn't announce all of his plans before this (until this later prophet disclosed some more of them), so that people wouldn't mistakenly think they had God all figured out.

Interpreters differ as to what these "new things" might be. The prophet may be referring to the way he has just identified Cyrus as God's specific instrument of deliverance. Or, he may be referring to his descriptions of the future servant figure, the Messiah, who will establish justice on earth. Whatever the case, the prophet will now be adding new predictions to the ones Isaiah made long before, in order to counteract both human self-confidence and dependence on idols—traits of the Babylonians that the captive Israelites have adopted!

➲ God has a crucial assignment for the exiles as his servants and messengers. He needs them to return to Jerusalem and become a beacon for all nations. But if they're ever to become part of a great enterprise like this, they first need to stop attributing God's work to other agents (like idols), and they need to stop priding themselves on their knowledge. How about you? Are you ready to step out if God calls you into a great enterprise? While still acknowledging secondary causes and intermediate agents, can you discern the hand of God at work in your life and surroundings? Are you prepared for God to involve you in new things that don't fit comfortably within your current framework of understanding?

4 Have someone read the next oracle, beginning with "Listen to me, Jacob, Israel, whom I have called" and ending with "'There is no peace,' says the Lord, 'for the wicked.'"

The prophet now offers a concluding challenge to the people. He reviews the arguments he's made so far: The Creator of the heavens and the earth has the right to accomplish his purposes through means of his own choosing, including the appointment of a pagan emperor as Israel's deliverer. The Lord has demonstrated his unique reality and discredited the idols by announcing his purposes in advance and carrying them out.

The prophet then asserts that he is a Spirit-filled messenger sent from God. In this role he has been foretelling new things, and now he forth-tells as well. He explains that the people have gone wrong in the past, but they can go right in the present if they will make a definitive choice for the LORD and against Babylon and its gods. He uses language drawn from the description in Psalm 78 of the exodus from Egypt, but also suggestive of the promise of a highway through the desert. He reminds the people of God's deliverance in the past ("they did not thirst when he led them through the deserts") and presents the challenge they must meet in their own generation: "Leave Babylon, flee from the Babylonians!" If they do, they will enjoy peace and well-being as dependable as the flow of a river, as steady as the breaking of waves on the shore. But if they continue in defiance and disobedience, their identity as Israelites will not exempt them from trouble. "There is no peace for the wicked."

➲ Here, as many times before, the prophet stresses that before anyone can take a daring step of obedience, they must put their trust exclusively in God. What percentage of your trust would you say is now in God, and what percentage is in other people and things? To measure trust another way, where would you put yourself on a scale where 10 is trusting God completely and 0 is not trusting God at all?

➲ What daring step of obedience, perhaps even one that would change your life forever, might God be calling you to take, just as he was calling the Judean exiles to leave Babylon and return to their homeland? What kind of work does God need to do in your life to bring you to the place where you will be willing and able to take this step? How can you cooperate with that work?

SESSION 20

THE PEOPLE REJECT THE PROPHET, BUT GOD EXPANDS HIS VOCATION

Book of Isaiah > Part Seven > Second Section

INTRODUCTION

So far in Part Seven of the book of Isaiah the prophet has proclaimed to his fellow Judean exiles in Babylon that the Lord wants to bring them back to their land so that they can be a messenger to all nations. The prophet has described how God wants to use the Persian emperor Cyrus as the instrument of this deliverance. He has pleaded with the people to trust in God—to believe that he hasn't abandoned them and is able to rescue them. All of this makes up the first section of Part Seven, which we have called the Rhapsody of Zion Redeemed.

The second section has a distinctly different character. The prophet now speaks very personally, telling his own story, as he describes how the people have rejected his message and even attacked him for proclaiming it. Nevertheless, he finds renewed strength and confidence when the Lord affirms his prophetic mission and shows him that it will ultimately have even more far-reaching effects than he has yet imagined. We'll begin reading and discussing the second section of Part Seven in this session.

READING AND DISCUSSION

1 Have someone read the next oracle in the book, beginning with "Listen to me, you islands; hear this, you distant nations" and ending with "because of the LORD, who is faithful, the Holy One of Israel, who has chosen you."

In this oracle the prophet describes how, when the people rejected his message, he despaired that all of his work had been in vain. But then, he reports, God reassured him that he still had a great work for him to do—indeed, greater than he ever imagined: God was sending him not just to "restore the tribes of Jacob" to faith, but to be a "light for the Gentiles" (that is, the non-Israelite nations), "that my salvation may reach to the ends of the earth." The prophet himself would, for the time being, take on the role of servant/Israel that the people were refusing to fulfill. Ultimately, God said, the rulers of the other nations would honor him, even though his own people had despised him. This is why the prophet addresses the "islands" and "distant nations" at the beginning of the oracle and introduces himself to them as their prophet, describing how God called him from birth and prepared him "like a sharpened sword" for this mission.

➲ What has God called you to do "from birth"? What indications were there even in your childhood that God had given you abilities and interests that pointed to a particular kind of service for him?

➲ How has God been "sharpening" you to fulfill this calling? For example, what skills, education, and training has he allowed you to acquire? What experiences has God brought into your life that have helped motivate and equip you to work in a certain field or with a certain group of people?

➲ The prophet was ready to give up when he met a major setback. But God told him that he wasn't finished yet; in fact, God still wanted to do much greater things through him. Do you know someone who has come back from an experience of disappointment and apparent failure to find an even stronger and clearer sense of vocation? If so, share their story with the group. Has something like this happened to you?

2 An extended oracle then depicts the fulfillment of the Lord's reassuring promises to the discouraged prophet: First the captive people of Israel are set free and returned to their land; then people from all nations come and join their community in such numbers that the Israelites (personified as Zion) wonder aloud where they've all come from.

But the exiles interrupt even these marvelous scenes with their doubts and disbelief. Zion laments, "The Lord has forsaken me, the Lord has forgotten me." And so God assures her in response that he would never do this. Even so, later in the oracle, the people wonder whether God can deliver them even if he wants to: "Can plunder be taken from warriors, or captives rescued from the fierce?" The Lord responds once more, describing his great power in language that evokes the exodus from Egypt ("I dry up the sea") and explaining that their defeat and exile were not the result of any lack of power on his part, but of their sins.

Have four people read this next oracle, beginning at these places:

- "This is what the Lord says: 'In the time of my favor I will answer you.'"
- "But Zion said, 'The Lord has forsaken me, the Lord has forgotten me.'"
- "Can plunder be taken from warriors, or captives be rescued from the fierce?"
- "This is what the Lord says: 'Where is your mother's certificate of divorce . . . ?'" (ending with, "I clothe the heavens with darkness and make sackcloth its covering").

➲ Picture in your mind what the successful fulfillment of your life mission would look like, as you understand it right now. Then picture God saying to you, "That's too small, there's a whole lot more I want to accomplish through you!" What would it look like for God to work through you so abundantly that you'd have to wonder, "Where did all this come from?"

➲ If you shared this expanded vision with other people, what objections might they raise to the idea that God wanted to do something like this through you, or even do it at all? How would you respond to these objections?

3 The next oracle is one of the most personal in the book. In it, the prophet describes how he has been mistreated by his own people for bringing them messages from God, and how he has nevertheless resolved to persevere in his mission ("I have set my face like flint"), whatever this might cost him. Have someone read this oracle, beginning with "The Sovereign Lord has given me a well-instructed tongue" and ending with "This is what you shall receive from my hand: You will lie down in torment."

We get a fascinating glimpse here into the prophet's life. We noted in session 15 how he seemed to receive his communications from God by hearing rather than by seeing. In this oracle he relates how God wakes him up each morning and has him listen to his word for that day. The prophet also describes the physical abuse he's suffered for delivering these messages: beatings on his back (perhaps some kind of community-sanctioned punishment) and the plucking out of his beard—both a painful torture and a degrading insult in this culture.

What has been his crime? Using the same kind of legal language that's found in several other parts of the book, the prophet challenges the people to make their case against him. There's no record of any response on their part. But it appears that because they've settled into the belief that God has abandoned them, and the prophet has had the audacity to challenge their complacent assumptions, they've accused him of misrepresenting God—of being a false prophet, for claiming that God wants to rescue them! This oracle is an answer to those accusations: The prophet records how he has faithfully fulfilled God's calling and he challenges his opponents to prove otherwise. He appeals to all those in the community who are sympathetic to his message to trust in the Lord, and he warns that those who try to walk by their own light will suffer in the end.

➲ Do you know anyone, or have you been told of anyone, who has suffered beatings, torture, or false accusations like this because of their service to God? If so, tell their story to the group. Then pray together for all the people that the group members mention and for followers of Jesus around the world who are being persecuted for their faith.

FOR FURTHER READING AND DISCUSSION

The next oracle in the book is a further word of encouragement to those members of the community who have believed the prophet's messages and who are waiting hopefully for God to act. Even though they are few in number and they're being threatened by the rest of their community, the prophet promises that God will work through them to renew the nation and proclaim his salvation throughout the world. Read this oracle, which begins, "Listen to me, you who pursue righteousness and who seek the LORD" and ends, "My righteousness will last forever, my salvation through all generations." Reflect on the situation it's describing. Try to put yourself in the place of those who have taken the prophet's instruction to heart, even though this means danger and uncertainty.

THE ARM OF THE LORD IS AWAKENED

Book of Isaiah > Part Seven > Second Section, Continued

INTRODUCTION

The prophet is eager to see the exiles freed. He also wants to be delivered personally from his persecutors. And so he calls on the "arm of the LORD" to wake up and do deeds of power as in the days of the exodus from Egypt (called "Rahab" here, as in session 10). The LORD responds by telling him he doesn't need to be afraid. He reminds him of his great power and reassures him of his calling ("I have put my words in your mouth"). In the preceding oracles the prophet's opponents appeared to be his fellow Israelites, since he could summon them to a community court proceeding. But here the people who are intimidating him are identified as oppressors whose prisoners will soon be set free. This probably means the Babylonians. It's likely that they were also persecuting the prophet, since he was declaring that Cyrus would imminently conquer them.

In the next oracle the LORD calls on Jerusalem to wake up. The city has been in a stupor ever since the Babylonian armies conquered it and carried its people away. But it's not primarily the daze of military defeat that Jerusalem must awaken from. Rather, its exiled citizens must wake up to the reality that it was their own injustice and oppression, not any failure of ability or willingness on God's part, that caused the city's destruction. They must also believe God's promises to forgive and restore them.

The LORD then calls to the city under another name, Zion, and once again tells it to wake up. This time he means that it must see itself not as a captive but as a splendid and beautiful restored community. The city's revival will restore God's good name, which has been defamed because of its citizens' disobedience and defeat. This oracle presents the image of Zion waiting eagerly for the news that the LORD is returning to dwell in her midst, and bursting into joyous song when this news arrives. At the end of this third oracle, in response to the earlier call for his arm to "awake," the LORD promises that he will "lay bare his holy arm" (that is, pull it out of his robe so he can use a sword or bow with it) and rescue his people.

Each of the three oracles in this series begins with the double imperative "Awake, awake." The last one ends with another double imperative: "Depart, depart!" The people must abandon the false security they've been finding in Babylon and its idols and instead embrace the daring adventure God is setting before them. They must return and rebuild Jerusalem and reestablish a temple there where people of all nations can come. They will bring "the articles of the LORD's house" back with them—some of the very treasures that Hezekiah showed the Babylonian envoys so many years before.

READING

Have different people read these three oracles out loud for the group. They begin at these places:

- "Awake, awake, arm of the LORD, clothe yourself with strength!"
- "Awake, awake! Rise up, Jerusalem."
- "Awake, awake, Zion, clothe yourself with strength!" (ending, "Depart, depart . . . the LORD will go before you, the God of Israel will be your rear guard").

DISCUSSION

➲ Was there a time when you were waiting hopefully and eagerly for good news and it arrived? If so, tell the group what this experience was like.

➲ The prophet finds hope by remembering the exodus. The Lord also encourages him by reminding him of his creative power. Can you find encouragement for the present by remembering occasions in the past when God delivered you from danger or provided for your urgent needs? What natural wonders have you seen that have spoken to you about God's creative power and love of beauty?

➲ The third oracle in this group shows that God's reputation in the world depends largely on his followers' obedience or disobedience. What have you seen followers of Jesus do in today's world that has helped to preserve or restore his good name?

➲ The messengers who come to Jerusalem proclaim peace, good tidings, and salvation. The Hebrew terms that are used here can describe situations in which everything is harmonious and in right relationship, in which people and things fulfill the purposes for which they were created, and in which people are freed from bondage of all kinds. Identify the situation in your personal or community life where you'd most like to see one of these ideals better realized and describe it for the group, using discretion to protect identities where appropriate. Then pray together for each of the situations that's mentioned.

➲ Conclude your time together, if you wish, by singing or listening to Lenny Smith's song "Our God Reigns," which is based on the last of the three oracles you read for this session and the first one you'll consider next time.

SESSION 22

THE SUFFERING SERVANT BRINGS SALVATION TO THE WORLD

Book of Isaiah > Part Seven > Second Section, Continued

INTRODUCTION

The prophet has called out "Awake, awake!" to the arm of the LORD, and God has said in response that he will pull his arm out of his robe and rescue the people. But what will this look like? The prophet is now given a further glimpse of what the coming servant figure, the Messiah, will do in the more distant future. (We know this is the future figure because when the prophet is speaking of himself as the servant, he says "I," but here he says "he," and refers to himself and the rest of the people as "us.") The prophet sees how the Messiah will bring a great deliverance to the whole world, far transcending the political liberation that Cyrus will bring to captive populations. Perhaps in part because of his own experiences of suffering and rejection *at the hands of* the people, the prophet is able to recognize how God will allow this future servant to suffer *on behalf of* the people, and how his painful experiences will become the means by which God brings about worldwide salvation.

The New Testament explains that Jesus fulfilled this prophecy and accomplished the purposes it describes when he died for us on the cross. In fact, the book of Luke-Acts records a conversation in which an important official of a foreign kingdom asks one of Jesus' followers, a man named Philip, to explain this prophecy. "Who is the prophet talking about," he asks, "himself or someone else?" Beginning with this passage, Philip tells the official the good news about Jesus. In response, the official comes to believe in Jesus and chooses to follow him.

READING

The oracle that describes the future servant's sufferings is composed in a form that Hebrew writers considered particularly beautiful and elegant, in which matched pairs are nested inside one another. This type of composition is known as a *chiasm*. In this case, the first and last stanza are matched, as are the second and fourth stanzas, while the middle one stands alone and presents the central message.

Have three people read this oracle out loud for the group. Assign them the letters A, B, and C and have them start reading at these places:

A. "See, my servant will act wisely."

  B. "Who has believed our message and to whom has the arm of the LORD been revealed?"

    C. "Surely he took up our pain and bore our suffering."

  B. "He was oppressed and afflicted, yet he did not open his mouth."

A. "Yet it was the LORD's will to crush him and cause him to suffer" (ending, "For he bore the sin of many, and made intercession for the transgressors").

DISCUSSION

1 In the first and last stanzas of this oracle (reading part A), the LORD is actually speaking, and so he refers to the Messiah as "my servant." He explains that what happens to him is ultimately the fulfillment of his own will and purposes. He also describes how the servant will be honored and rewarded for what he does. Just as people will be appalled by his humiliation and sufferings, they will be amazed by his exaltation. The servant will be "raised and lifted up"—the same words used to describe the LORD in Isaiah's vision in the temple. "After he has suffered, he will see the light of life." When understood in retrospect in light of Jesus' experiences, these words seem to predict his resurrection from the dead and his exaltation into the presence of God. (Other lines in this oracle seem to predict the same, for example, "I will give him a portion among the great . . . because he poured out his life unto death.")

Throughout this study guide we've stressed the importance of recognizing how the primary (initial) meaning of the prophecies in the book of Isaiah is for the places and times in which they were spoken. But in this case, the description of the Messiah's sufferings and exaltation appears to be one of the "new things," one of the events coming in the future, that the prophet has said he will announce to demonstrate the unique reality of the God of Israel (session 19). The many correspondences in detail between these words and Jesus' experiences, and their explanation of the meaning and purpose of his death, provide prophetic testimony to his identity as the Messiah.

➲ If there are people in your group who know the story of Jesus, have them explain how these parts of the prophecy were fulfilled in his life and death:

- He was held in low esteem.
- He was innocent of saying or doing anything wrong.
- He did not open his mouth.
- He was punished and wounded.
- He was pierced for our transgressions.
- His grave was with the rich.
- After he suffered, he saw the light of life.

2 In the second and fourth stanzas of this oracle (reading part B), the prophet meditates on the unexpected character of the Messiah.

For one thing, he comes in humility. He doesn't make a grand entrance on the world stage, like a conquering general or royal heir apparent. Instead, he grows up unobtrusively, like a "tender shoot." He seems so ordinary that people "despise" him. This Hebrew term doesn't mean that he is hated, but rather that people think little of him—they "held him in low esteem." He doesn't seem at all like the "arm of the Lord," and so the prophet wonders who will ever believe this message about him.

For another thing, the Messiah willingly suffers injustice. He doesn't protest when he's wrongly accused, convicted, and sentenced to death. While the role of God's prophetic agents is ordinarily to denounce injustice, in this case the future servant allows it against himself without a word of protest, even though he is completely innocent. He is led silently "like a lamb to the slaughter," and so he becomes, as the New Testament prophet John the Baptist described Jesus, the "lamb of God who takes away the sin of the world."

➲ Where in your life, your community, or the world have you discovered that God was at work in something (or someone) that initially seemed so inconsequential you would never have expected this? In other words, what seemingly insignificant events, opportunities, relationships, trends, etc. have turned out in the end to be important channels of God's work in you and around you?

➲ How can a follower of Jesus today tell the difference between those times when they're supposed to fight against injustice and those times when they're supposed to accept injustices against themselves as a way of continuing the work that Jesus began?

3 The middle stanza of this oracle (reading part C) describes the essence of the Messiah's work. The prophet has already declared, at the opening of the Rhapsody of Zion Redeemed, that the specific sins of idolatry, injustice, and oppression that caused Israel's exile have been paid for. But a deeper and more universal problem still remains. All people have gone astray from God and turned to their own ways. This means that they have refused to honor their Creator's intentions for how they should live and abandoned the relationship of loyalty and devotion they should have with God. They have tried instead to direct their own lives, and as a result they have spread destruction and brokenness throughout the world.

The prophet foresees that to bring healing, forgiveness, and reconciliation into this situation, the Messiah will voluntarily accept the consequences that we who have rebelled against God should experience instead: pain, suffering, guilt, abandonment, destruction. Because he takes on these consequences, we are delivered from them. "The punishment that brought us peace was on him, and by his wounds we are healed."

➲ Work together as a group to explain how, through his sufferings and death, Jesus took on the punishment we deserved for turning away from God and made it possible for us to be reconciled with God. Give each person in the group the chance to share, if they wish, how they have responded to what Jesus has done for them. Perhaps someone has not been a follower of Jesus but wants to become one now that they understand more about his sufferings and death. Help them do this by having them pray to God with other group members and then give a public testimony of their faith in Jesus in a public setting such as a worship gathering.

SESSION 23

GOD PROCLAIMS RECONCILIATION TO ISRAEL AND THE WORLD

Book of Isaiah > Part Seven > Second Section, Concluded

INTRODUCTION

Part Seven of the book of Isaiah concludes with two oracles that proclaim and celebrate the reconciliation that God wants to have with all people. This reconciliation, as we saw last time, will be achieved definitively through the future work of the Messiah, the Suffering Servant. But even now, as God forgives the exiles and restores them to their home, they can have a foretaste of the salvation that will one day become worldwide. However, this means they will have to leave behind their settled lives in Babylon, abandon the idols they've come to worship, and renew their trust in God to lead them into a seemingly precarious future.

READING AND DISCUSSION

1 Have someone read the next oracle in the book, beginning with "Sing, barren woman, you who never bore a child" and ending with, "'This is the heritage of the servants of the Lord, and this is their vindication from me,' declares the Lord."

This oracle presents two extended images to describe how God will forgive and rescue the people. It first uses the restoration of a marriage as a symbol of reconciliation. The LORD speaks to an unnamed woman (who is probably Zion, emblematic of the nation, since that city is then addressed directly). He tells her that while she is now alone and childless, soon he will take her back as his wife and she will have so many children she will have to make extra room for them. The oracle then envisions the city rebuilt with dazzling precious stones. This represents the splendor of the peace and justice that will prevail in the restored community. There are echoes here of the oracles in which Jerusalem and Zion were told to awaken, but now, in light of the future servant's reconciling work, the vision is even more splendid and expansive.

➲ If your own community were transformed into a place of peace and righteousness, how would things be different from the way they are now?

➲ What examples can you give of relationships that you've seen reconciled? Do you know of friends who became alienated but were then reconciled . . . family members whose relationship was severely strained but was then healed . . . married couples who were once struggling, separated, or divorced who now have a restored marriage that's stronger and healthier? What made the difference in these situations? Pray together as a group for troubled relationships that you know about. (People can speak simply of "my friends" if necessary in order to protect identities.)

➲ The unnamed woman is told to enlarge her tent right away, in anticipation of what the Lord will do for her. Have you ever felt led to act in the present in order to be ready for what God was going to do in your life in the near future? If so, tell your story to the group.

2 Have someone read the next oracle, beginning with "Come, all you who are thirsty, come to the waters" and ending with, "This will be for the Lord's renown, for an everlasting sign, that will endure forever."

With this oracle, Part Seven closes with a final exhortation to the people. The Lord speaks first, calling on them to come to him and enjoy "the richest of fare" freely, "without money and without cost." He doesn't primarily mean actual food, although he has promised throughout this part of the book that he will provide for their needs. Rather, he wants them to hear, understand, and embrace his offer to renew his covenant with them, so that they can be restored to their land and be a "witness to the peoples" there.

The prophet speaks next, calling on his fellow exiles one more time to "turn to the Lord" and receive his forgiveness. Finally, the Lord speaks again, assuring the people that while they may not always understand what he is doing, his purposes will be accomplished as surely as the rain and snow water the ground and make the plants grow.

The oracle ends with a reprise of an image that has recurred throughout Part Seven, that of a highway through the desert that will allow the exiles to return home. Now, as the Israelites travel this route, the desert shrubs are transformed into hardwood trees that clap their hands in celebration. The mountains and hills burst into singing. This is the joy that God is inviting his people to experience in a restored relationship with him.

➲ What are one or two of the most memorable unexpected free meals you've enjoyed? Share your stories with the group.

➲ What things do the people in your culture spend their money on that don't really satisfy? What is God offering here that will be truly satisfying?

➲ When God refers here to the word that goes out from his mouth that will achieve the purpose for which he sends it, this probably means, in this context, his decree that the exiles will be allowed to return to their land. But the statement is often applied more generally to God's Word in the form of the Bible, in which the purposes that he has announced throughout the course of his relationship with humanity have been collected. Where do you see the Scriptures at work in the world today, bearing fruit and accomplishing God's purposes?

FOR FURTHER READING AND DISCUSSION

Part Five of the book of Isaiah also ends with an oracle that depicts a highway through the desert. In session 1 you noted where Part Five begins. Find this place again and skim forward a page or two until you reach where it says, "The desert and the parched land will be glad." Read through to the end of Part Five. Note how this oracle develops some of the same themes and uses some of the same images you've become familiar with in Part Seven. (When the book of Isaiah was put together in its present form, this oracle was probably placed here to help create continuity between the two halves of the book.) What additional ideas and symbols does this oracle present?

AFTER THE RETURN FROM EXILE

SESSION 24

ANOTHER NEW PROPHET CALLS THE RETURNED EXILES TO JUSTICE AND HOPE

Book of Isaiah > Part Eight > First Section

INTRODUCTION

The rest of the book of Isaiah, Part Eight, speaks to a situation some years after the one addressed in Part Seven. God's promises through the prophet have begun to be fulfilled: The Persian emperor Cyrus has conquered Babylon and allowed the Jewish exiles to return home and start rebuilding Jerusalem. However, much still needs to happen within the community of returned exiles before it can fulfill the rest of God's promises by becoming a witness to all nations of his glory and love. The people are falling back into the same sins of idolatry, oppression, and injustice that led God to take them away from the land in the first place. Many are worshipping the Lord once again, but only through outward forms, not from the depths of their hearts. And so a further prophetic word is needed to call the people who have returned to their land to return wholeheartedly to their covenant relationship with God.

Who spoke this prophetic word? As we noted in session 14, while some interpreters hold that Isaiah the son of Amoz was responsible for all of the oracles in the book that bears his name, others believe that a later prophet spoke the words in Part Seven of the book. Among those interpreters, some think that this same prophet traveled back to Jerusalem with the returning exiles and continued to speak to them there. Others hold that a third prophet arose within the community and delivered the oracles in Part Eight. The debate among biblical scholars is ongoing, and good arguments can be made for each of these positions. But for reasons that will be explained in this session, this study guide will follow the interpretation that a third prophet is responsible for the final part of the book of Isaiah. Once again we'll refer to him simply as "the prophet."

READING AND DISCUSSION

1 Find the beginning of Part Eight and skim forward a couple of pages until you reach the place where it says, "And it will be said: 'Build up, build up, prepare the road!'" Have someone read the short oracle that begins there, ending with, "'There is no peace,' says my God, 'for the wicked.'" Then have someone read the following oracle, beginning with, "Shout it aloud, do not hold back," and ending with, "For the mouth of the LORD has spoken."

One good reason to believe that a new prophet is speaking in this new setting is that these two oracles seem to depict his calling, in language and imagery that echoes the calling of his predecessors. (The account of this prophet's calling, like Isaiah's, has been placed in the middle of his first oracles.) The LORD is described as "high and exalted" and "holy," in the exact language that Isaiah used in his temple vision. Just as an unidentified voice called out to the prophet in Babylon to prepare a way for the people back to their homeland, so an unidentified voice calls out to this prophet to prepare a road for the people back to their God. And just as the earlier prophet was told, as he was being called, to cry out and lift up his voice with a shout, so this prophet is told to shout aloud and raise (lift up) his voice as he is given the assignment to "declare to my people their rebellion and to the descendants of Jacob their sins." By echoing words, phrases, and symbols from earlier in the book, this prophet, too, is stressing the continuity between the preceding oracles and his own. You'll notice many more examples of this as you read through Part Eight. (For example, the first oracle you read ends with exactly the same words as the Rhapsody of Zion Redeemed.)

➲ To begin calling the people back to God, the prophet speaks of his holiness and exaltation, but he also describes how ready God is to forgive and restore those who are lowly and contrite—that is, those who humbly admit what they've done wrong and express sorrow for it. Do you think of God as someone who's eager to forgive you and welcome you back if you're genuinely sorry for the wrong things you've done? Why or why not? (What has been modeled for you by people who've represented God in your life?)

➲ The prophet describes the peace that people experience when they're forgiven. But he also depicts the inner state of those who don't ask for forgiveness as "like the tossing sea, which cannot rest, whose waves cast up mire and mud." The principle seems to be that we keep remembering the wrong things we've done until we are forgiven for them, but then after that, they shouldn't keep troubling us. What advice would you give someone who had done something wrong, asked and received forgiveness from God and all the people affected, but then still couldn't get it out of their head? If God wants forgiven people to enjoy peace, where might these accusations be coming from?

2 The second oracle you read speaks to the practical struggles of the returned exiles. They're trying to rebuild cities and homes that have long been lying in ruins, but so far they haven't become prosperous enough to do this. They're asking for God's help and even fasting (going without food) to demonstrate the urgency of their appeal. But God is not listening to them, the prophet says, because even in the midst of their religious observances they're oppressing rather than helping the poor and needy in their community. If they will turn from injustice and oppression to care for those in need, and if they will once again observe the Sabbath as a holy and honorable day (as the law requires), God will strengthen and prosper them, and they'll succeed in rebuilding.

➲ Have you ever gone without food for religious purposes? If so, what were those purposes? Tell the group what your experience was like.

➲ Do you regularly observe a time of Sabbath in your life, for rest, reflection, and worship? If so, tell the group how you do this.

➲ Fasting and Sabbath-keeping are examples of spiritual disciplines, time-honored practices that people use intentionally and regularly to strengthen their life of devotion to God. The prophet says here, however, that the kind of fasting God really wants is to "loose the chains of injustice." As a group, discuss the relationship between spiritual disciplines and activities that promote justice. Under what circumstances might these two types of practices seem to come into conflict, so that we would have to choose one over the other? (For example, can you share your meal with the hungry if you're fasting?) Under what circumstances can these practices inform and strengthen each other? Give specific illustrations of how they would do this.

3 Turn back to the beginning of Part Eight and have someone read the first oracle, which begins, "This is what the LORD says: 'Maintain justice and do what is right,'" and ends, "I will gather still others to them besides those already gathered."

Among the returned exiles are two groups who, according to the Law of Moses, should be excluded from full participation in the life of the community, most notably from its worship:

- Those of foreign descent. Because certain foreign nations refused to help the Israelites when they came out of Egypt as refugees, their descendants were excluded from the community.
- Eunuchs. The law forbade anyone who became a eunuch from entering the sanctuary in order to stamp out the pagan practice of offering one's manhood to the goddess Astarte. The returned exiles who are eunuchs, however, were made so through castration in order to serve in the Babylonian court.

The prophet declares that these exclusions will no longer apply. So long as a person will hold fast to God's covenant, honoring him both through religious observances such as Sabbath-keeping and by maintaining justice, they will be welcomed and blessed.

➲ In this culture, a person's "name" (meaning their lasting reputation and legacy, their social footprint) came largely through having a great clan of descendants. But God promises the eunuchs, who can't have children, "a memorial and a name better than sons and daughters" in the form of a permanent place within his temple, likely meaning that they will live forever in his presence. In your culture, in what ways does a person get a large and lasting social footprint? How do people feel, and how are they made to feel, when they don't achieve this? In light of this prophecy, what do you think God would say to such people?

➲ The foreigners who embrace God's covenant are not only welcomed into the community and its life of worship, but they are actually allowed to serve in the sanctuary and offer sacrifices—privileges that the Law of Moses granted only to the priests and Levites. Here the prophet envisions the most complete possible fulfillment of the earlier statements that people from all nations would come to worship God in Jerusalem. (There's a similar vision at the end of the book, when God says he will choose some people from all the nations to be priests and Levites.) If you're a member of a community of Jesus' followers, tell the group who in your community is allowed to serve the Lord's Supper and baptize new believers. Does a person have to be ordained or certified in some way to do these things? Or can anyone who is a believer and a member of the community in good standing do one or both of them? What reasons are given for either approach?

FOR FURTHER READING AND DISCUSSION

Read the oracle that comes right after the one you've just considered, beginning with "Come, all you beasts of the field" and ending with, "Whoever takes refuge in me will inherit the land and possess my holy mountain." What more do you learn from this oracle about the conditions within the community of returned exiles? What oracles in the first half of the book does this one recall? How could the people go through the experience of conquest, exile, and dramatic return, then still go back to their old ways to this extent?

Read the oracle that comes right after the two you considered at the start of this session, beginning with "Surely the arm of the LORD is not too short to save" and ending with "'My Spirit, who is on you, will not depart from you, and my words that I have put in your mouth will always be on your lips . . . from this time on and forever,' says the LORD." In this oracle the prophet explains once again that God has not been helping the people because of their sins of injustice and oppression. But he also describes how, for lack of any person to act on his behalf, the LORD himself will come and establish justice. Do you think God ordinarily expects to act through human agents, and is "appalled" when no one steps forward? What does it look like when God acts directly? How do you understand the promise that's made to the prophet at the end of this oracle?

SESSION 25

THE RESTORED JERUSALEM IS ENVISIONED AS A BEACON FOR THE NATIONS

Book of Isaiah > Part Eight > Second Section

INTRODUCTION

Part Eight of the book of Isaiah now moves into a second section that has a distinctly different character from its first section. Instead of admonishing the people for their injustice and oppression, the prophet paints a glorious picture of a restored and purified Jerusalem serving as a beacon for the nations. For the first time this prophet speaks in the first person (saying "I" and "my") as he reflects on the privilege of his calling. He expresses his resolution to keep prophesying and praying until God's purposes are accomplished.

READING AND DISCUSSION

1 Each of the three oracles in this section is in the form of a *chiasm.* (This form was explained in session 22.) Have three people read the first oracle. Assign them the letters A, B, and C and have them start reading at these places:

A. "Arise, shine, for your light has come, and the glory of the LORD rises upon you."

  B. "Who are these that fly along like clouds, like doves to their nests?"

C. “Foreigners will rebuild your walls, and their kings will serve you.”

B. “The glory of Lebanon will come to you.”

A. “Although you have been forsaken and hated” (ending, “I am the LORD; in its time I will do this swiftly”).

The two passages in part A describe how the restored city will shine with a bright, attractive light and how the treasures of the nations will be brought to Jerusalem as gifts and offerings as Zion’s lost children are carried home. The two passages in part B describe how the people of two specific places will bring their distinctive gifts. And the passage in part C brings a central promise from God: The city will be rebuilt and remain open perpetually for people from all nations.

This oracle is spoken to Zion, the “City of the LORD.” It echoes the oracle in Part Seven that describes her sons and daughters streaming home in such numbers that she wonders, “Where have all these come from?” In both oracles the prophets envision a future time when the people of God will become a multinational community lit by the LORD’s brilliant presence. Many interpreters believe that this prophecy is already being fulfilled in a figurative way as people from around the world become followers of Jesus, swelling the community’s numbers and bringing in the distinctive gifts of their cultures and individual personalities. Many interpreters also believe that this prophecy will be fulfilled more literally when Jesus returns to earth to rule in righteousness and peace.

➲ How have you seen the community of Jesus’ followers enriched by the gifts of people from different cultures and nationalities?

➲ Do you tend to picture prophecies like this one being fulfilled more figuratively, within history, or more literally, at the end of history? Why?

2 Have three people read the next oracle, starting at these places:

A. "The Spirit of the Sovereign LORD is on me."

B. "They will rebuild the ancient ruins."

C. "Instead of your shame you will receive a double portion."

B. "For I, the LORD, love justice."

A. "I delight greatly in the LORD" (ending, "the Sovereign LORD will make righteousness and praise spring up before all nations").

Note the repeated images of festive clothing and growing plants in part A, the nations' recognition of Zion's children in part B, and the central promise from God in part C.

Despite the many problems of the community (which you considered in the previous session), in this oracle the prophet rejoices that he has been called to proclaim a message of hope within this difficult situation. He describes how God has given him his Spirit to equip and empower him for this work, just as the prophet in Babylon said, "The Sovereign LORD has sent me, endowed with his Spirit," and just as Isaiah described how the Spirit of the LORD would rest upon the coming Messiah. This prophet believes and expects that through his ministry, peace and justice will be reestablished within the community and that the cities devastated a generation before will be rebuilt.

Jesus read the opening words of this oracle out loud in the synagogue of his hometown of Nazareth and then announced, "Today this scripture is fulfilled in your hearing." (Recall from session 3 that when words spoken at earlier points in the unfolding story of God take on a fuller and deeper meaning in light of later developments in that story, they are said to be fulfilled.) Jesus was using this prophet's words to announce and celebrate how he himself had been empowered by the Spirit and to explain how his mission was a vastly greater extension of the prophet's calling to make Jerusalem a light to all nations.

➲ What do you think it means for a follower of Jesus today to be filled with God's Spirit? Is this something that every believer is meant to experience? Or is it only for people who are given special assignments? How can a person know, like these prophets, that God's Spirit is resting upon them?

➲ Have you ever been involved in rebuilding "ruined cities that have been devastated," or do you know anyone who has? If so, tell the group something about this. Was this an individual effort, or done with a church or some other organization? How long did it last, or is it still ongoing? What conditions had to be created within the community in order for rebuilding to begin successfully? Pray together as a group for those who are involved in renewing urban neighborhoods near you.

3 Have three people read the next oracle, starting at these places:

A. "For Zion's sake I will not keep silent."

B. "I have posted watchmen on your walls, Jerusalem."

C. "The LORD has sworn by his right hand."

B. "Pass through, pass through the gates!"

A. "The LORD has made proclamation to the ends of the earth" (ending, "you will be called Sought After, the City No Longer Deserted").

Note the new names the city is given in both passages in part A, and the references to the city's walls and gates in part B. Also note that part C once again presents a promise from God.

In this oracle the prophet resolves to keep speaking to the community about God, and to God about the community, until Jerusalem becomes a beacon to the nations. In the previous two oracles Zion was called deserted ("forsaken") and desolate (NIV "devastated"), but in this oracle it is given wonderful new names: Hephzibah, "My delight is in you"; Beulah, "married"; Sought After; No Longer Deserted. As noted in session 3, people in this culture could be given another name as the result of some important event in their life.

To see this marvelous transformation accomplished, the prophet enlists others to join him in the work of intercession. He posts these collaborators figuratively on the walls of Jerusalem as watchmen and tells them not to rest as they call on the Lord to fulfill his purposes. (This is a pointed contrast to the description of blind and silent watchmen in the first oracle that was recommended for further reading in the previous session.)

This oracle concludes with language that echoes this prophet's calling: "Build up, build up," "prepare the way." This language also echoes the calling of the prophet in Babylon. It repeats the highway imagery, it includes a command to tell Zion that her God is coming, and it ends with the announcement, "See, his reward is with him, and his recompense accompanies him." The prophet remembers his own calling, and he takes renewed inspiration from the work of his predecessor, in order to strengthen his resolution to continue praying and prophesying.

➲ When the prophet addresses his watchers as "you who call on the Lord," he describes them literally as "you who remind the Lord." The idea is that these people who are committed to praying for the community are supposed to know what God has promised and remind God of those promises and "give him no rest" until he acts. Is it respectful to address God as if he needs to be reminded to keep his promises?

➲ The watchers described here are also like the ones in the oracle that begins "Awake, awake, Zion." They watch for signs of God coming to fulfill his purposes. Do you know of any groups of people who look together for signs of God's activity in the world and then support that activity in prayer? Would you like to be part of such a group?

➲ Do you believe that God has called you to try to accomplish a particular purpose during your time here on earth? If so, to encourage yourself in the pursuit of that purpose, as the prophet does here, recall the time or times when you first sensed that calling. Describe this calling for the group if you're comfortable doing so.

SESSION 26

THE PROPHET PRAYS FOR THE NATION AND GOD RENEWS HIS PROMISES

Book of Isaiah > Part Eight > Third Section

INTRODUCTION

The third section of Part Eight of the book of Isaiah is similar in character to the first section. While there are still some promises of restoration and renewal, in much of this section the prophet once again threatens the people with divine judgment for their idolatry and wickedness. This third section begins with a description of how God looked for someone to help his people, but saw no one, and so achieved salvation by his own arm. This description uses exactly the same language found at the end of the first section. This gives Part Eight the overall shape of a chiasm:

First Section: Judgment

God acts alone to bring salvation

Second Section: Promise

God acts alone to bring salvation

Third Section: Judgment

This arrangement is an elegant way to conclude the entire book.

READING AND DISCUSSION

1 The first oracle in this section depicts God's victory over his enemies in graphic, even gory, imagery. Have someone who's comfortable with difficult material read this oracle out loud for the group, beginning with, "Who is this coming from Edom?" and ending with "in my wrath I . . . poured their blood on the ground."

There was longstanding hostility between Israel and the country of Edom. The Edomites even captured Israelites who had escaped from the destruction of Jerusalem and turned them back over to the Babylonians to be executed or enslaved. And so Edom is used to represent all of Israel's enemies in prophecies like this one that envision worldwide judgment. (The first oracle in Part Five similarly uses Edom as a symbol for all of Israel's enemies. You may wish to read it now or at the end of this session for a comparison.)

This prophecy uses a question-and-answer format that's common in Hebrew song and poetry. But one of the questions here—"Why are your garments red, like those of one treading the winepress?"—has a shocking answer. As this winepress image from the natural world is interpreted in terms of the human world, it turns out that the wine is actually blood: God's garments are stained and spattered with the blood of his opponents, whom he has torn apart. The emphasis in this oracle is on how much God cares for those who trust in him, so that he will act to save them from injustice and oppression even if he must do so alone. Still, it's difficult to come to terms with this gruesome picture.

➲ What place do images like this one have in the Bible?

➲ Here wine is used as a symbol of the blood of God's opponents, who have been destroyed for their wickedness. In the Lord's Supper, wine is used as a symbol of the blood of Jesus. Does this oracle give us some idea of what Jesus experienced on the cross when he accepted the penalty from God for our own wickedness?

2 The next passage in this section is actually composed like a psalm of supplication in which someone prays on behalf of the whole community for forgiveness and restoration.[1] Psalms 79 and 80 are examples of this kind

1. To find out more about the various types of psalms in the Bible, see the study guide in this series to Psalms, Lamentations, and the Song of Songs.

of psalm; they too are prayers for God to restore the nation after its destruction by the Babylonians. Psalm 89 is an even closer parallel: It begins quite similarly, and it, too, includes a lengthy historical section. Have four people read the following parts of this passage, which represent the basic elements of a psalm of supplication, beginning at the places indicated:

- Recollection: "I will tell of the kindnesses of the LORD"
- Complaint: "Look down from heaven and see"
- Appeal: "Oh, that you would rend the heavens and come down"
- Confession: "All of us have become like one who is unclean"
- Renewed Appeal: "Yet you, LORD, are our Father" (ending, "Will you keep silent and punish us beyond measure?")

It would have been unusual for a prophet to lead the community in prayer to God. It was much more typical for prophets to speak to the people in God's name. So here the prophet may be quoting a psalm of supplication taken from the community's worship in order to respond to the psalm in his next oracle. On the other hand, the prophet has just said that he won't cease praying for Jerusalem until God acts. So it is actually possible that the prophet himself composed this psalm and that it represents the kind of prayer he offered for the nation as it struggled to rebuild its cities and temple. In either case, as we'll see under the next point, the following oracle is a response to the cry for help in this psalm.

➲ On what grounds does the author of this psalm ask for God's help? That is, for what reasons should God forgive and restore the people, even though they've continually disobeyed? In your prayers, can you ask God to help your community on similar grounds?

➲ The psalm says of God's people, "In all their distress he too was distressed." Do you think of God becoming distressed for you when you get into trouble? Why or why not?

➲ The psalm asks, "Why, Lord, do you make us wander from your ways and harden our hearts so we do not revere you?" How do you understand this language? Choose the answer that best expresses your thoughts, or give another of your own:

a. The psalmist is saying that it feels as if God actually wants the people to be estranged from him, since he hasn't come to help them.

b. This is one of several places where the Bible asserts that God deliberately hardens the hearts of some people because he hasn't chosen them to be saved.

c. This phrase is describing the results of God's judgments against the people, not his intentions toward them: Because God hasn't come back to rescue them yet, they're wandering away.

3 In the next oracle in this section, God, speaking through the prophet, responds to the appeals for help in the psalm of supplication. Have someone read this oracle, beginning with, "I revealed myself to those who did not ask for me" and ending with "For the past troubles will be forgotten and hidden from my eyes."

While the psalm implores God to "look on us . . . for we are all your people," this oracle responds that many in the community are actually not God's people—not in the sense of worshipping and serving him loyally and exclusively. Instead, they're walking "in ways not good" and worshipping idols, trying to communicate with the dead, and ceremonially eating unclean things in pursuit of magical powers. (You heard about practices like these in the readings for session 24.) God actually began reaching out to the people long before they asked for help, but he hasn't rescued them yet because of their continual rebellion. The defiant members need to be purged from the community so that God can deliver the faithful remnant.

The promises to the remnant here recall the oracles in the previous section of Part Eight. There Jerusalem was told it would be given new names and no longer be called Desolate; while the psalm of supplication laments that Jerusalem is still a desolation, this oracle promises that the Lord will give his servants another name.

The language and imagery of this oracle also recall the closing oracle of Part Seven:

- The prophet in Babylon urged the exiles to "seek the LORD while he may be found." Here God promises blessings "for my people who seek me."
- The earlier prophet invited his hungry and thirsty hearers to eat and drink without price. This prophet, drawing on the same imagery, warns that only God's faithful servants will eat and drink, while those who continue to rebel will go hungry and thirsty.
- The members of the faithful remnant are described repeatedly as God's servants, echoing the term that's used evocatively throughout Part Seven.

The language and imagery reach even farther back into the book: The grape cluster recalls Isaiah's song of the vineyard and his own agricultural images for the remnant. While words and symbols are echoed throughout the book, the allusions become more dense and conspicuous as the book draws to a close.

➲ This oracle explains that God looks for us long before we start looking for him, so that if his help is delayed, this may be because of our disobedience. However, it may also be because we need to wait on God, as other parts of the book often say. How can a person recognize the cause of a delay and so respond appropriately, either by confessing and forsaking the wrong things they're doing, or else by waiting patiently and trustingly?

4 The next oracle in this section echoes earlier oracles in the book even more vividly. Have someone read it for the group, beginning with "See, I will create new heavens and a new earth," and ending with, "'They will neither harm nor destroy on all my holy mountain,' says the LORD."

In this oracle Jerusalem is not just rebuilt and restored, it's recreated afresh, along with the entire heavens and earth. The blessedness of its citizens is described in language that evokes the central promise of the last oracle you considered in session 25, in which God promised that his people would always enjoy the fruits of their own labor. But even more strikingly, this oracle quotes directly from Isaiah's vision of how the Messiah will establish justice and righteousness throughout the world (session 12), so that in the natural world even predators like wolves and lions will live peacefully with animals that are usually their prey. Here the prophet, through the Spirit who rests upon him and through the words of his predecessors, is enabled to see beyond God's immediate purposes for his community and glimpse the time when, to fulfill his ultimate purposes, God will renew the entire creation. All sorrows will end and people will live on and on in the presence of God, at peace with the world around them.

➲ How do you picture the fulfillment of God's ultimate purposes for the created world? Does everything here get destroyed, and God's people go off somewhere else for eternity? Or does everything here get renewed, so that the most noble and beautiful aspects of this creation endure forever as a home for those who love God?

FOR FURTHER READING AND DISCUSSION

The next oracle in this section describes the situation of the returned exiles in more detail: They're trying to rebuild the temple as a house and resting place for God. Some Israelites are obedient to the word of the Lord through this prophet, and they're being hated and excluded by their own people as a result. God reassures them that he values their loyalty more than the ritual sacrifices the rest of the community is offering.

The next oracle echoes an image from earlier in the book and depicts Zion as a mother nurturing her returned children.

The last passage in the book (which is prose rather than poetry) offers another description of the nations streaming to Jerusalem to worship the Lord. It ends with an ominous prediction of judgment against those who rebel against God.

➲ Conclude your time together, if you wish, by singing or listening to Brian Doerksen's song "Resting Place," which is based on the opening lines of the oracle about the returned exiles trying to rebuild the temple.

THE AUTHORSHIP OF ISAIAH

Here's a brief glimpse into the scholarly conversation about the authorship of Isaiah.

Those who believe that Isaiah spoke all of the words in the book that bears his name note that:

1. Within the book, none of the contents are ascribed to any other figure, while in three places they are attributed to Isaiah: twice at the start of Part One, and again at the start of Part Two.

2. In the New Testament, all the quotations from both halves of the book are said to be from Isaiah.

3. There are great similarities in language, imagery, and message between the two halves.

4. It's doubtful that anyone who composed and delivered oracles of such beauty and power as are found in the second half of the book could have remained anonymous.

5. No Christian interpreters challenged the idea of single authorship until the modern period, when some began to doubt that the ancient Hebrew prophets could predict details of the future (for example, that the emperor who would free the Judean captives would be named Cyrus). Because of their bias against predictive prophecy, these interpreters attributed thc part of the book that addresses the later time period to someone who lived then. This is how the theory of multiple authorship originated in Christian circles.

Those who believe that the book is a collection of oracles both by Isaiah and at least one later prophet respond to these arguments by noting:

1. That other biblical collections, such as Zechariah and Psalms, are made up of materials ascribed to known authors as well as materials whose authors are not named.

2. When the words of unnamed authors are quoted in the New Testament, they are referenced by the name of the main author of the collection in which they appear. For example, in the book of Acts, the words of the unattributed second psalm are said to have been spoken by David.

3. A later prophet who knew and believed in Isaiah's prediction that the Judeans would return from exile, and who wanted to identify himself as a contemporary herald of that promise, would have intentionally echoed Isaiah's language and imagery in his own oracles. This would be particularly true if he had found not just spiritual but also literary inspiration in the earlier prophet's words. Ancient writers and artists did not place such a great premium on originality as their counterparts do today. Instead, they paid tribute to their teachers and models by imitating their works, even as they put their own personal imprint on their creations. Traditional Chinese painting provides a good example of this approach.

4. It is admittedly difficult to imagine that anyone could have created such magnificent poetry as is found in the second half of Isaiah and still remained anonymous. Nevertheless, there are other great works of world literature whose authors are not known to us, including several other compositions within the Bible, such as Job. But we must certainly admire the humility and sacrificial spirit of anyone who had such powerful literary gifts but nevertheless subordinated his own identity to that of the prophet whose promises he wished his community to recognize and embrace as their fulfillments began to dawn.

5. Ascribing the second half of the book of Isaiah to a later prophet does not necessarily rule out belief in the possibility of predictive prophecy. Quite the contrary: Entering into this part of the book fully on its own terms requires a devout reader to share this belief with the speaker. This is necessary to appreciate his argument that the Lord should be worshipped instead of the idols of the nations since he alone revealed in advance what was going to happen, "So we could say, 'He was right.'" It's also necessary to believe

in the possibility of prediction to accept this prophet's claim that he himself is going to declare "new things . . . before they spring into being." Jewish scholars embraced the idea of multiple authorship on internal grounds many centuries before some Christian scholars began to question the possibility of predictive prophecy.

The debate between these two positions is ongoing, but either position can be held by someone who believes in the inspiration and authority of the Bible as the Word of God.